In Rem Foreclosure

Forms and Procedures

2016

Christopher B. McLaughlin

Access Free Foreclosure Forms

Purchase of this book includes FREE access to forms designed to help you navigate the *in rem* tax foreclosure process. The forms come in both Microsoft Word and PDF format in a zip file.

Visit the URL below to access and download your forms today:

sog.unc.edu/pubs/9781560118589

For information about other publications and resources from the School of Government, visit **sog.unc.edu**.

Electronic download available

UNC | SCHOOL OF GOVERNMENT

The School of Government at the University of North Carolina at Chapel Hill works to improve the lives of North Carolinians by engaging in practical scholarship that helps public officials and citizens understand and improve state and local government. Established in 1931 as the Institute of Government, the School provides educational, advisory, and research services for state and local governments. The School of Government is also home to a nationally ranked Master of Public Administration program, the North Carolina Judicial College, and specialized centers focused on community and economic development, information technology, and environmental finance.

As the largest university-based local government training, advisory, and research organization in the United States, the School of Government offers up to 200 courses, webinars, and specialized conferences for more than 12,000 public officials each year. In addition, faculty members annually publish approximately 50 books, manuals, reports, articles, bulletins, and other print and online content related to state and local government. The School also produces the *Daily Bulletin Online* each day the General Assembly is in session, reporting on activities for members of the legislature and others who need to follow the course of legislation.

Operating support for the School of Government's programs and activities comes from many sources, including state appropriations, local government membership dues, private contributions, publication sales, course fees, and service contracts.

Visit sog.unc.edu or call 919.966.5381 for more information on the School's courses, publications, programs, and services.

Michael R. Smith, DEAN
Thomas H. Thornburg, SENIOR ASSOCIATE DEAN
Frayda S. Bluestein, ASSOCIATE DEAN FOR FACULTY DEVELOPMENT
Bradley G. Volk, ASSOCIATE DEAN FOR ADMINISTRATION

FACULTY

Whitney Afonso	James M. Markham
Trey Allen	Christopher B. McLaughlin
Gregory S. Allison	Kara A. Millonzi
David N. Ammons	Jill D. Moore
Ann M. Anderson	Jonathan Q. Morgan
Maureen Berner	Ricardo S. Morse
Mark F. Botts	C. Tyler Mulligan
Peg Carlson	Kimberly L. Nelson
Leisha DeHart-Davis	David W. Owens
Shea Riggsbee Denning	LaToya B. Powell
Sara DePasquale	William C. Rivenbark
James C. Drennan	Dale J. Roenigk
Richard D. Ducker	John Rubin
Joseph S. Ferrell	Jessica Smith
Alyson A. Grine	Meredith Smith
Norma Houston	Carl W. Stenberg III
Cheryl Daniels Howell	John B. Stephens
Jeffrey A. Hughes	Charles Szypszak
Willow S. Jacobson	Shannon H. Tufts
Robert P. Joyce	Vaughn Mamlin Upshaw
Diane M. Juffras	Aimee N. Wall
Dona G. Lewandowski	Jeffrey B. Welty
Adam Lovelady	Richard B. Whisnant

Printed in the United States of America
21 20 19 18 17   02 03 04 05 06
ISBN 978-1-56011-858-9

Contents

List of Forms

Preface and Acknowledgments

This publication is intended to serve as a guidebook for the growing number of counties and municipalities that are using the *in rem* foreclosure process to collect property taxes and other debts owed to local governments that are secured by liens on real property. It replaces the portions of William A. Campbell's *Property Tax Lien Foreclosure: Forms and Procedures* (6th ed. 2003) that concern *in rem* foreclosures.

The author is indebted to Professor Campbell for creating the foundation upon which this new publication rests. Equally important were the contributions of Valerie Curry, the deputy collections manager for the Orange County Tax Administration. By sharing invaluable practical insights on many of the issues discussed in the following pages, Ms. Curry greatly improved this publication.

Thanks are also offered to editor Melissa Twomey and her talented colleagues in the School of Government's Publications Division. Without their input and creativity this unique multi-media publication would not have been possible.

Christopher B. McLaughlin
Chapel Hill
April 2016

In Rem Foreclosure: Forms and Procedures

I. Overview and Constitutionality

The Machinery Act[1] describes the *in rem* tax foreclosure procedure in Chapter 105, Section 375 of the North Carolina General Statutes (hereinafter G.S.) as a "simple and inexpensive" alternative to the full-blown civil action required by the "mortgage-style" foreclosure procedure in G.S. 105-374. That description might be overly optimistic in light of the diligent title search and notification efforts tax offices undertake before starting the foreclosure process. But it is true that *in rem* foreclosures are usually quicker and cheaper than mortgage-style foreclosures because they can be accomplished without attorneys and without the more onerous pleading and service requirements of civil litigation.

In a nutshell, the *in rem* procedure permits a local government to docket a judgment against real property for delinquent taxes and proceed with an execution sale of the property three months later. In contrast, a mortgage-style foreclosure usually takes between six months and a year to get to sale.

A. Judicial Scrutiny

The expedited nature of *in rem* foreclosures has been the source of numerous court challenges to the process in its sixty-plus-year history. Property owners and lienholders have repeatedly alleged that the *in rem* procedure fails to provide constitutionally adequate notice to interested parties before property is sold and their interests terminated.[2] Despite the many legal challenges, the *in rem* foreclosure process remains good law.

The process has evolved over time, though, sometimes in response to litigation that identified weaknesses in the *in rem* procedure. For example, the relevant statute originally required that notice be provided only to the taxpayer who originally listed the property for taxation, even if that taxpayer

---

1. Chapter 105, Subchapter II of the North Carolina General Statutes (hereinafter G.S.).

2. *See, e.g.*, Henderson Cty. v. Osteen, 292 N.C. 692 (1977) (failure to give notice of sale to property owner invalidates foreclosure sale); Hardy v. Moore Cty., 133 N.C. App. 321 (1999) (county satisfied notice provisions by sending registered mail to taxpayer's last known address and advertising sale; county not required to call the country club to which the property was related in order to obtain taxpayer's new address); Jenkins v. Richmond Cty., 99 N.C. App. 717 (1990) (failure to send individual notice to all known property owners invalidated foreclosure); Murray v. Cumberland Cty., 98 N.C. App. 143 (1990) (foreclosure void because county had information necessary to make personal service and failed to do so); Town of Cary v. Stallings, 97 N.C. App. 484 (1990) (foreclosure invalid because city knew that property owner no longer resided at old address and failed to make personal service on owner); Annas v. Davis, 40 N.C. App. 51 (1979) (sheriff's failure to send personal notice to property owner voided foreclosure sale).

no longer owned the property. The statute now requires that notice be given to the current owner of the property, a much more logical and constitutionally sound approach.

Additional amendments to the statute were motivated by court rulings in other jurisdictions. Most notable was the 1983 U.S. Supreme Court decision in *Mennonite Board of Missions v. Adams*[3] that struck down part of a similar Indiana tax foreclosure statute because it did not require that notice be provided to lienholders. The Court held that lienholders, like property owners, must be notified by that form of "notice reasonably calculated, under all circumstances" to inform the lienholder of the government's intent to deprive that party of a property interest.[4] After *Mennonite*, lienholders such as mortgagees are entitled to notice of the foreclosure by mail rather than simply by publication if their addresses can be easily obtained.[5]

In addition to challenging the *in rem* statute itself, property owners have also attacked the execution sale procedure required for *in rem* foreclosures.[6] G.S. 105-375(i) mandates that the real property being foreclosed upon be sold "by the sheriff in the same manner as other real property is sold under execution," subject to a few procedural changes unique to *in rem* sales. Execution sales are governed by Article 29B of G.S. Chapter 1.

In 2008, the North Carolina Court of Appeals rejected multiple challenges to the execution sale of a beachfront condominium on Topsail Island in *St. Regis of Onslow County v. Johnson*.[7] The condo had been sold between the docketing of the judgment and the foreclosure sale. Both the former and the new owners of the condo claimed that it was unconstitutional for the sheriff not to provide each of them with personal notice prior to the sale.

The court disagreed. First, it dealt with the former owner, who had received personal notice of the judgment but not of the sale. G.S. 1-339.54, which creates the notice requirements for an execution sale, requires personal notice of the sale only to property owners who live in the county where the sale will occur. Nonresident property owners are entitled only to notice sent via registered mail to the property owner's last known address. Although the sheriff mailed notice to the property owner prior to the sale, the property owner never received it. The unclaimed registered mail was returned to the sheriff months after the sale.

The court found that constitutional due process concerns did not require personal notice before the sale. It was enough for the sheriff to attempt to provide notice via registered mail in addition to posting notice on the property and publishing notice of the sale in the local newspaper. The combination of these actions was "reasonably calculated" to provide the property owner with notice of the pending sale, as required by the U.S. Supreme Court in *Mennonite*.

Next, the court dealt with the new owner, who took title after judgment was docketed but before the execution sale. The sheriff did not provide personal notice to the new owner prior to the sale. Not needed, said the court. Because the judgment was docketed before the new owner took title, the new

---

3. 462 U.S. 791 (1983).

4. *Id.* at 795.

5. For a summary of amendments to the *in rem* procedure made in 2006 and the judicial decisions that led to those changes, see Andrew H. Werbrock, *The Constitutionality of North Carolina's Tax Foreclosure Procedure after* Jones v. Flowers, PROP. TAX BULL. No. 140 (UNC School of Government, Nov. 2006), http://sogpubs.unc.edu/electronicversions/pdfs/ptb140.pdf.

6. "Execution" in this context refers to the enforcement of a judgment for money against the defendant, not capital punishment.

7. 191 N.C. App. 516 (2008). Although this case involved a judgment obtained by a private party (a condominium owners' association), the legal analysis and holding applies to *in rem* judgments because it utilizes the same execution sale provisions.

owner was on notice that the property was subject to a lien ripe for execution and sale. The new owner had the information it needed to protect its interest in the property; the lack of additional notice in the form of personal service was not a constitutional violation.

The *St. Regis* court's spirited affirmation of the execution sales process should provide great comfort to local governments who use *in rem* foreclosure. Two years later, the court of appeals provided an even stronger affirmation of the *in rem* foreclosure process in its 2010 *Mai v. Carolina Holdings, Inc.* decision.[8]

The *Mai* case involved an *in rem* foreclosure sale conducted by the city of Charlotte for unpaid demolition costs.[9] Carolina Holdings held a separate lien on the property in question.

As required by G.S. 105-375, the city sent letters to the property owner and to Carolina Holdings prior to docketing a judgment against the property. Months later, the city mailed notice of the sale to the property owner but not to Carolina Holdings, in accord with the statute's requirements. The city also published notice of the sale in a local newspaper. Carolina Holdings claimed it didn't learn of the sale to Mai until a full year later. It then challenged the *in rem* procedure in court alleging that the failure to provide personal notice to lienholders of record violates the Due Process Clauses of the United States and North Carolina constitutions.

Carolina Holding's argument fell on deaf ears. The court found that the *Mennonite* standard was more than satisfied by G.S. 105-375's requirement that lienholders receive notice of the intent to docket a judgment via registered or certified mail months before a foreclosure sale.

Relying on language from a 1976 North Carolina Supreme Court case, *Henderson County v. Osteen*,[10] that spoke approvingly of the *in rem* procedure, the court concluded that the absence of a second notice to lienholders prior to the actual foreclosure sale does not render the entire process constitutionally inadequate: "[N]otice [under [G.S. 105-375]] . . . would, in our opinion, be sufficient to satisfy the fundamental concept of due process of law and, therefore, to comply with Article 1, § 19, of the Constitution of North Carolina and the Due Process Clause of the Fourteenth Amendment of the Constitution of the United States."[11] Essentially, the court found that Carolina Holdings ignored the initial notice of the foreclosure at its peril and could not legitimately complain that it was harmed by its failure to learn of the specific sale date.

The importance of the *Mai* decision lies not only in its substantive holding—it's okay to mail a single notice to lienholders—but also in its unqualified adoption of the N.C. Supreme Court's language in *Osteen* that previously was viewed as non-binding "dicta" and not as a conclusive blessing of the *in rem* foreclosure procedure.

Courts surely will continue to scrutinize *in rem* foreclosures to ensure that local governments dot all of their i's and cross all of their t's. And it is always good practice to go beyond the minimum required notice when it can be done without great effort or cost—e.g., send a second notice to lienholders if you have their addresses. But in general, as of 2015 the *in rem* procedure stands on solid constitutional ground.

---

8. 205 N.C. App. 659 (2010).

9. Demolition costs relating to housing code enforcement actions can be collected using property tax remedies, including the *in rem* foreclosure remedy. *See* G.S. 160A-443 *and* Christopher B. McLaughlin, *Beyond the Property Tax: Collecting Other Taxes and Fees*, Prop. Tax Bull. No. 162 (UNC School of Government, Feb. 2011), http://sogpubs.unc.edu/electronicversions/pdfs/ptb162.pdf.

10. 292 N.C. 692 (1977).

11. *Mai*, 205 N.C. App at 665 (quoting *Osteen*, 292 N.C. at 708).

B. Title Concerns

The *in rem* foreclosure process has recently come under attack from some title insurance companies and attorneys. These critics claim that courts are quick to overturn *in rem* sales based on concerns about the notice given to owners and lienholders during the *in rem* process. The problem, according to these critics, is the poor title search process implemented by tax offices pursuing *in rem* foreclosure. They also argue that the limited availability of title insurance for properties sold at *in rem* foreclosures suppresses the sale prices of these properties, impairs their resale value, and, consequently, harms local governments' real property tax bases.

A search of recent judicial opinions and discussions with property tax officials who have been using *in rem* foreclosure for decades suggests that concerns about the quality of title obtained in this process are overblown.

There is no evidence that courts are more likely to overturn *in rem* foreclosure sales than mortgage-style foreclosure sales due to notice concerns. Despite the hundreds, if not thousands, of *in rem* foreclosures across the state in the past few decades, the author could find only a single appellate case in which an *in rem* foreclosure was overturned for improper notice in the past thirty-plus years.

In *Howell v. Treece,*[12] the Richmond County tax office moved to foreclose on unoccupied timber land owned by a South Carolina resident. The tax office knew the land was unoccupied and had a copy of the deed granting title to the taxpayer that listed a South Carolina address for the taxpayer. Regardless, the tax office had been sending tax bills for the timber land to the taxpayer in care of the Richmond County town in which the timber land was located for several years, with the post office always returning the bills with an "addressee unknown" notation. Even worse, when preparing for the *in rem* foreclosure, the tax office again sent notice only to the taxpayer in care of the town. The tax office did not publish notice of the foreclosure or take any additional steps to locate and notify the taxpayer about the pending foreclosure. The taxpayer did not learn of the foreclosure until several years later when she attempted to obtain a loan against the timber land. Not surprisingly, the taxpayer convinced the court to overturn the *in rem* foreclosure on the grounds of insufficient notice.

If *in rem* foreclosures were as risky as their critics claim, North Carolina's courts should be full of cases like *Howell.* That case arose in 1984. The fact that it is the only case in more than three decades to invalidate an *in rem* foreclosure on notice grounds is strong evidence that *in rem* foreclosures are now prosecuted much more carefully by tax offices and are no more risky than "regular" mortgage-style foreclosures under G.S. 105-374.

In fact, the very few appellate cases from recent years in which courts have invalidated tax foreclosure sales based on inadequate notice all involve mortgage-style foreclosures. See, for example, *County of Jackson v. Moor*[13] and *County of Durham v. Daye.*[14] In *Moor,* the county was foreclosing on property owned jointly by a husband and wife. Service was made on the husband at his place of employment but not on the wife. The fact that the wife was aware of the foreclosure did not excuse the county's failure to actually serve her. In *Daye,* the county attempted to serve unknown heirs by publication but never gave notice of the foreclosure to the tenants living in the house being foreclosed upon and never asked those tenants if they knew how to contact the property owners (which they did).

These cases emphasize a lesson that experienced tax collectors already know: notice is extremely important in a tax foreclosure regardless of the process being used. The city or county must use

---

12. 70 N.C. App. 322 (1984).

13. ___ N.C. App. ___, 765 S.E.2d 122 (2014) (unpublished).

14. 195 N.C. App. 527 (2009).

extreme care to identify and notify all parties with interests in the property being foreclosed upon. It's irrelevant whether the foreclosure is a mortgage-style proceeding overseen by an attorney or an *in rem* proceeding run by tax office employees; without a diligent effort to locate and serve all owners and lienholders, any type of foreclosure runs the risk of a successful legal challenge.

Feedback from local tax collectors confirms this research: courts rarely overturn *in rem* tax foreclosure sales. Multiple veteran tax collectors, each with fifteen-plus years of experience, report that they have yet to see a single *in rem* foreclosure sale successfully challenged in court. This may be due to the fact that tax collectors have learned from past mistakes and now do much better jobs of locating and serving all parties with interests in the properties being foreclosed upon.

The second argument raised by *in rem* critics is that properties sold at *in rem* foreclosure sales are negatively impacting county tax bases due to title insurance problems.

It's true that title insurers have concerns about properties purchased at *in rem* foreclosure sales. Here is a comment from an experienced title attorney:

> *I can confirm that we often are unwilling or unable to provide title insurance for tax foreclosures generally, but especially in rem foreclosures, without substantial due diligence, if at all. We do worry about whether the city, county, or attorney handling the tax foreclosure ha[s] done adequate research to identify, locate, and personally serve all owners of any interest in the property—fee, life tenant, heirs, remaindermen, contingent remaindermen, lienholders, mortgagees, etc. With a civil action foreclosure, this must be "vetted" by a judge before the final entry, rather than just a unilateral judgment being filed without any third party oversight. Having the blessing of a judge that all has been properly done, notice clearly researched and given, etc. goes a long, long way toward assuring marketability of the properties and the titles.*[15]

This view, which no doubt is shared by other title attorneys, seems to be based on a misunderstanding of the *in rem* process.

Service of notice on owners and lienholders is usually accomplished in the same manner regardless of whether the foreclosure is *in rem* or "regular" mortgage style. Both foreclosure procedures permit service via registered or certified mail, return receipt requested.[16] Both procedures require additional efforts if service via mail fails, including posting notice on the property and publishing notice in the newspaper for at least two weeks.

The argument that a judge "blesses" service in a mortgage-style foreclosure doesn't hold water. In both types of proceedings, the county will be required to provide the court proof of service, including publication if required. So long as that proof is provided, a judge will not investigate the adequacy of service any more than the clerk of superior court will in an *in rem* proceeding.

As for identifying all potential owners and heirs, there is no basis for believing that an attorney prosecuting a mortgage-style foreclosure will be any more diligent in a title search than will a paralegal or other tax office employee pursuing an *in rem* foreclosure. In fact, the reverse may be true. An attorney working on a fixed-fee arrangement for local tax foreclosures has a disincentive to spend any more time than the bare minimum on a title search—that attorney is not getting paid more if she spends more time on the case. And as is true of service issues, judges do not routinely investigate the adequacy of a title search in a mortgage-style foreclosure. Nearly all mortgage-style foreclosures are

---

15. Email from Nancy Short Ferguson, state counsel for Fidelity National Title Group and vice president and senior state counsel for Chicago Title, to author (Nov. 14, 2015).
16. G.S. 105-374(c); 1A-1, Rule 4; 105-375(c)(3).

uncontested and resolved without trial or other substantive inquiry from a judge. The properties that get to foreclosure are almost always properties that the owners have essentially abandoned.

Regardless, it's clear that title insurers have concerns about *in rem* foreclosure property. But do those concerns lead to lower sale prices and decreases in local governments' tax bases? The evidence suggests otherwise.

First, tax collectors often see repeat buyers at their foreclosure sales. If these buyers were having trouble insuring or re-selling *in rem* properties, they would not continue to buy them.

Second, appraisers generally do not take forced sales such as foreclosure sales into account when assigning tax values. Even if the *in rem* sale price is less than the property would have produced at a voluntary, arms-length transaction, it should not have an effect on the property's tax appraisal.

Third, the properties that actually make it to foreclosure sale are almost always low-value properties on which taxes have not been paid in years. Even if a property's tax appraisal decreased after an *in rem* sale, the net effect on the local government's tax revenue will still be positive if the new owner is more diligent about paying taxes on the property than the old owner.

Fourth, and most importantly, very few *in rem* foreclosures actually make it to sale. Case in point: Valerie Curry of the Orange County Tax Office has overseen many hundreds of *in rem* foreclosures, and she reports that more than 80 percent of those foreclosures are terminated due to payment prior to sale. Markus Kinrade, revenue director for Wake County, sees similar results.

Much of an *in rem* foreclosure program's value lies in its ability to produce payment from delinquent taxpayers with just the threat of a sale, not the actual sale. All of the objections to *in rem* foreclosures deal with post-sale issues. That's a concern for something less than 20 percent of all *in rem* foreclosures. The small minority of properties that do make it to sale have such low ownership interest and low values that judicial challenges and title problems are unlikely to have any substantive impact on the local government down the road.

Critics of the *in rem* process argue that local governments should always use the mortgage-style foreclosure process (G.S. 105-374) rather than *in rem* because they can collect the related attorneys' fees from the sale proceeds. That argument ignores two important problems.

First, attorneys' fees may be charged to the taxpayer in a mortgage-style foreclosure only if the complaint is filed.[17] If the taxpayer pays the delinquent taxes before the complaint is filed (as often happens once the taxpayer realizes foreclosure is likely), then the local government will be stuck with the tab for the attorney's title search and other pre-complaint work.

Second, many of the properties that make it to foreclosure sale won't produce enough sale proceeds to cover both the delinquent taxes and the attorneys' fees. Once again, the local government will be stuck with the attorney's tab.

While local governments should not abandon the use of *in rem* foreclosure, they can take steps in the *in rem* process to lessen concerns about these properties. The first and most important step is to work very hard to identify all potential owners and to serve those potential owners with notice of the foreclosure. See section VI, below, for more on the title search process. The second step is to insist that the clerk of court open a file for the *in rem* proceeding and include in that file all relevant title search and service documentation provided by the local government. Often there are no court files for *in rem* foreclosures available for review by title insurance companies. This lack of documenta-

---

17. G.S. 105-374(i). For more details on attorneys' fees in mortgage-style foreclosures, see Chris McLaughlin, *Property Tax Foreclosures: Attorneys' Fees and Interest*, Coates' Canons: NC Local Gov't L. Blog (UNC School of Government, May 14, 2015), http://canons.sog.unc.edu/?p=8087.

tion concerning the tax office's effort to locate and serve all property owners contributes greatly to title insurers' worries about *in rem* properties. Making sure that a well-documented file exists at the courthouse may help convince title insurers that the property is not a major insurance risk.

II. The Foreclosure Decision

Tax collectors are obligated by statute to "employ all lawful means" to collect their local governments' property taxes.[18] This provision implicitly obligates local governments to use the foreclosure remedy when available and necessary.

Some local governments are hesitant to use foreclosure, which is perhaps the strongest of all of those lawful means. These governments might be worried about the administrative and financial aspects of the process or about the negative publicity that might arise if they wind up evicting residents from their homes.

These concerns are understandable but outweighed by the harm caused by the government's refusal to use what might be the only effective remedy to collect certain taxes. The property tax system becomes less equitable when some taxpayers are permitted to ignore their tax obligations with no negative consequences. Collection rates and public confidence in the tax system are sure to drop as a result.

These statutory and public policy concerns lead to only one reasonable conclusion: local governments should at least consider the use of foreclosure on every property subject to a tax lien when other collection remedies fail. That said, there are some legitimate reasons—most of them financial—why a local government might choose not to foreclose on a particular property.

Below are a few questions for tax officials and their governing boards to ask as they consider moving forward with a foreclosure.

1. Have all other collection remedies been exhausted?

Foreclosure eliminates all other remedies for property tax collection.[19] If the tax collector believes that another remedy—levy and sale or attachment and garnishment—is likely to be successful to satisfy the tax debt, the best approach is to try those other remedies first. A tax collector can use those remedies as many times as needed and as practical to satisfy a particular tax debt. Multiple levies and attachments may be in place simultaneously for a single outstanding tax. But once a tax collector begins the foreclosure process, she must terminate all of those other remedies.

2. Will the property attract bids high enough to cover the taxes and costs?

If a property is of such marginal value that it's unlikely to attract bidders willing to pay at least as much as is owed on the property, foreclosure may not make sense. Knowing this fact, the tax office needs to investigate the potential market value of the property before taking any other steps toward foreclosure. This process might involve physically inspecting the property, finding relevant

---

18. G.S. 105-350(1).

19. G.S. 105-366(b) states that collection remedies against personal property, levy and sale under G.S. 105-367 and attachment and garnishment under G.S. 105-368, may be used "[a]t any time after taxes are delinquent and before the filing of a tax foreclosure complaint under G.S. 105-374 or the docketing of a judgment for taxes under G.S. 105-375." As a result, once a foreclosure complaint is filed or a foreclosure judgment is docketed, the local government loses the ability to target the taxpayer's personal property to collect the taxes included in the foreclosure.

comparable sales, and consulting with local real estate professionals. In some cases, the size and location of the property make it likely that the only bidders would be the owners of neighboring properties. Contacting these individuals will be key to determining whether foreclosure is viable.

3. Is the local government willing to sell the property at cost to a new buyer or take ownership of the property?

Even if pre-foreclosure market research suggests that a sale of the property won't produce enough funds to cover the taxes and costs owed, foreclosure still could make sense. The local government might be willing to sacrifice the delinquent taxes to get the property in the hands of a new owner who is more likely to stay current on future taxes. Or the local government might be willing to purchase the property at the foreclosure sale by use of its own bid at the amount of taxes and costs owed on the property.[20] If no other bidder tops that bid, then the local government becomes the owner. It can keep the property for public use or sell it later under the rules governing the disposal of surplus real property.[21] See section XIV, below, for more details on a local government's obligations when it purchases property at a tax foreclosure sale.

4. Are there other liens on the property that are senior to the property tax lien?

Senior liens get paid from foreclosure sale proceeds before junior liens. The foreclosure of a senior lien extinguishes all junior liens on the same property. As a result, senior liens present obstacles to foreclosure but junior liens do not.

Happily for local tax collectors, local government property tax liens are generally senior to all other liens on real property.[22] Mortgage liens, the most common lien found on real property besides property tax liens, are always junior to real property liens and therefore should never be a barrier to pursuing foreclosure.[23] The same is true of federal tax liens.[24]

The only lien that might give a tax collector pause would be a state tax lien for income taxes or any other state-levied taxes. Local government property tax liens are "first-in-time, first-in-right" with state tax liens, meaning whichever lien attaches to the property first is senior and gets paid first.[25] State tax liens attach when recorded with a register of deeds or docketed with the appropriate superior court. Real property tax liens arise and attach on each January 1.

As a result, a state tax lien is likely senior to a local property tax lien if the state recorded or docketed its lien prior to January 1 of the earliest year for which delinquent property taxes are owed on the foreclosure property. In this case, foreclosure may not make sense for a local government if the state tax lien exceeds the likely sale price of the property. Some local governments have had success negotiating with the N.C. Department of Revenue to relinquish its lien priority so that sale proceeds can be shared more equally. But if that is not possible, foreclosure will not be a great option for the

---

20. See section X.D.1, below, for more on setting a "minimum bid" for a foreclosure sale.

21. See G.S. 105-376 and section XIV, below, for more on the responsibilities of a local government that purchases property at a tax foreclosure sale.

22. For more details on the priority of liens, see Christopher B. McLaughlin, *Fundamentals of Property Tax Collection Law in North Carolina* (UNC School of Government, 2011) (hereinafter *Fundamentals*), chapter 5.

23. G.S. 105-355(b)(1). In fact, the presence of a mortgage lien makes it more likely that a foreclosure or the threat of foreclosure will produce payment of the delinquent taxes. Because mortgage lenders know their liens will be extinguished and eliminated if the tax foreclosure goes to sale, they will usually pay the delinquent taxes and costs immediately upon learning of a foreclosure action.

24. 26 U.S.C. § 6323.

25. *See* Carteret Cty. v. Long, 349 N.C. 285 (1998), G.S. 105-356(a)(1), *and* G.S. 105-241(d).

local government because it is extremely unlikely the sale will produce enough funds to satisfy the delinquent property taxes.

5. Would a foreclosure sale of the property create unusual public relations concerns?

Tax collection is meant to be an objective and equitable process in which all similarly situated taxpayers are treated similarly. Foreclosure should be a remedy for all taxes on all real property that cannot be collected using other means and for which there are no financial obstacles such as those described above.

But very occasionally subjective concerns might make foreclosure a bad option for the local government. The facts involved with a particular delinquent tax account might lead a reasonable tax collector to conclude that the local government would be best served by avoiding foreclosure, at least temporarily.

Perhaps the tax office had been mailing the tax bills to an incorrect address. Perhaps the taxpayer had been escrowing tax payments with her mortgage company and that company absconded with that money and left the taxpayer in the lurch. One could imagine a variety of scenarios in which foreclosure is legally and financially feasible but not the wisest course of action at the present moment.

Instead, the tax office might want to consider a payment plan with the taxpayer, even if that plan extends beyond the usual time period for such plans.[26] The local government might have to wait longer to get paid than it would in a foreclosure action, but the public relations benefits could likely outweigh the minor financial loss.

6. Should the foreclosure be pursued jointly with another local government?

When a property is being foreclosed upon, taxes are often owed to multiple jurisdictions; it's unusual for a taxpayer to become delinquent on county taxes but not city taxes, or vice versa. A local government pursuing *in rem* foreclosure against a property must always consult with other taxing units having jurisdiction over the property to learn if there are any outstanding property tax liens on the property. If this is the case, the local government that initiates the foreclosure has a decision to make concerning how much it involves the other local government in the *in rem* process.[27]

---

26. A payment plan is simply an agreement between the taxpayer and the tax office under which the taxpayer agrees to pay a certain amount per week or per month toward delinquent taxes. In return, the tax office agrees not to pursue enforced collections (attachment and garnishment, foreclosure, etc.) so long as the taxpayer makes the promised payments. Although the Machinery Act does not specifically authorize payments plans, it does grant tax collectors the flexibility to decide when to initiate enforced collection remedies. That flexibility allows for the use of payment plans. Tax collectors who offer payment plans should be sure to obtain information that will expedite the use of enforced collection remedies if the taxpayer violates the agreement; a Social Security number, bank account details, and name and address of an employer should be required from the taxpayer before the payment plan is finalized. Tax collectors also must remember that Machinery Act interest must continue to accrue on all delinquent amounts; the Machinery Act does not authorize tax collectors to waive or suspend interest while a payment plan is in effect. It is unclear whether a payment plan may extend beyond the ten-year statute of limitations for property tax enforced collections (including *in rem* foreclosures), but it seems likely. The statute of limitations created by G.S. 105-378 is an affirmative defense that must be raised by the taxpayer to defeat a belated collection action. Presumably, the taxpayer could choose to waive that defense in return for a payment plan. If so, then a local government could still pursue *in rem* foreclosure after the ten-year statute of limitations if a payment plan specifically authorized late collection actions.

27. In a mortgage-style foreclosure, there is less flexibility with regard to other taxing units. Any taxing unit that has a tax lien on the property being foreclosed upon must be made a party to the action. The only decision is whether the local governments will jointly prosecute the foreclosure as co-plaintiffs or if one local government will be named as the plaintiff and the others named as co-defendants with the taxpayer.

Ideally, the two governments would discuss the issue beforehand and agree to prosecute the foreclosure jointly. Tax liens from multiple taxing units can be consolidated and docketed together as one judgment.[28] The property can then be sold for the benefit of all the taxing units with tax liens on the property and they would share in the proceeds proportionately. See section XIV.F, below, for more details on post-sale procedures.

If the city and the county do not initially agree to move ahead jointly, then the foreclosing government must give notice to the other taxing units with liens on the property just as it does to all other lienholders. The government receiving notice of the foreclosure could choose to begin its own *in rem* foreclosure, in which case the judgments could be combined for one execution and sale.[29] The proceeds would then be shared between the two governments as if they had pursued the foreclosure jointly from the start.

But what if one local government gives notice of an *in rem* foreclosure to another and that second government fails to respond? In that case, the foreclosing government may still move forward with its *in rem* foreclosure but will be forced to sell the property subject to the other local government's tax liens. Because tax liens held by different local governments are all of equal dignity and equal priority, the foreclosure of one local government's tax lien does not extinguish a tax lien held by another local government that was not included in the docketed judgment.[30]

For example, assume Blue Devil City and Carolina County both hold liens for delinquent property taxes on Parcel A owned by Wanda Wolfpack. The city's tax lien is $3,000, the county's is $5,000. Carolina County initiates the *in rem* process after attempting and failing to get Blue Devil City's agreement to foreclose jointly on Parcel A. The county sends the required notice to Blue Devil City, which fails to respond. If the *in rem* foreclosure proceeds to sale, the county will be required to sell Parcel A subject to Blue Devil City's $3,000 tax lien. This will likely discourage potential bidders—who wants to buy a property that might be foreclosed upon immediately by another local government?—and will definitely reduce the price a bidder would offer because the winning bidder would become personally responsible for the $3,000 city tax bill.[31]

7. Should the foreclosure include other debts owed to the local government?

Machinery Act collection remedies such as foreclosure were initially created for the collection of local property taxes but have been expanded in reach to cover other types of debts owed to local governments.[32] The Machinery Act's mortgage-style foreclosure and *in rem* foreclosure remedies may be used to enforce the liens on real property that arise under special assessments,[33] nuisance abatement

---

Regardless, the end result will be the same: all taxing units will share in the proceeds of the foreclosure, unless a particular taxing unit fails to respond to the foreclosure complaint. *See* G.S. 105-374(c), (h).

28. G.S. 105-375(k).

29. *Id.*

30. *See* G.S. 105-356(a)(2) (making all local government tax liens of equal dignity and priority) *and* 105-375(g) (stating that the property shall be sold free and clear of all liens except tax liens not included in the judgment).

31. G.S. 105-365.1(b)(1) (owner on date of delinquency and all subsequent owners are personally responsible for taxes on real property).

32. *See Fundamentals*, chapter 15, for a full discussion of when and how Machinery Act remedies may be used to collect other taxes and fees owed to local governments.

33. G.S. 153A-195 (counties) and 160A-233(a) (municipalities).

costs,[34] minimum housing code enforcement costs,[35] ambulance service fees,[36] and possibly solid waste fees.[37] Although these liens do not have quite the same "super-priority" that local property tax liens possess, they are granted payment preference over most competing liens.[38]

Tax collectors may include both property taxes and these other non-tax debts in the same foreclosure if they are all liens on the same property. If a foreclosure includes no property taxes and only special assessments, nuisance abatement costs, or minimum housing code enforcement costs, then the tax collector need not advertise the liens prior to beginning the foreclosure, as is required for property tax liens.[39] All other notice requirements remain the same regardless of the type of lien being foreclosed.

8. *In Rem* or Mortgage Style?

After a local government has reviewed all of the questions above and decided to move forward with foreclosure, the final question is, "Which type of foreclosure is best for this property?" Unfortunately there is no easy answer to this question. *In rem* is generally cheaper and quicker than a mortgage-style foreclosure under G.S. 105-374 but does raise some title concerns. As discussed above, those concerns seem a bit overblown, but they continue to exist.

The one situation in which it might be best to avoid *in rem* foreclosure is when the property in question has a high value and is certain to attract bids sufficient to cover the costs of that attorney-driven procedure. Although the risk of a reversal is generally very small for *in rem* foreclosures when care is taken during the process, that risk could increase for high-value properties because disgruntled former owners (or alleged owners) have more motivation to sue. In such cases, mortgage-style foreclosure might be the best option, especially when it is clear that the property will attract bids high enough to cover the associated attorneys' fees. But otherwise, *in rem* foreclosure can be an effective and efficient collection method when undertaken with great care and diligence.

III. *In Rem* Foreclosure and Bankruptcy

A federal bankruptcy filing can present many challenges to a local tax collector.[40] But it does not always mean that the taxes owed by the debtor will never be collected. Most often, a bankruptcy filing will delay but not entirely prevent an *in rem* foreclosure against the debtor's property.

Here's why: an "automatic stay" arises immediately upon the filing of a bankruptcy petition. The stay prohibits any enforced collection efforts against the taxpayer/debtor while the bankruptcy is

---

34. G.S. 153A-140 (counties) and 160A-193 (municipalities).

35. G.S. 160A-443 (applicable to both counties and municipalities).

36. G.S. Ch. 44, Arts. 9A and 9B (applicable to both counties and municipalities).

37. If billed with property taxes. G.S. 153A-292 and -293 (counties) and 160A-314 and -314.1 (municipalities).

38. For a full explanation of property tax lien priority, see *Fundamentals*, ch. 5.

39. G.S. 105-375(e) explicitly waives the advertising requirement for special assessments. Although neither the Machinery Act nor the authorizing provisions for nuisance abatement and housing code enforcement do the same, the author believes that those debts are similarly exempt from the advertising requirement. Those debts are not property taxes, and only property tax liens are required to be advertised annually under G.S. 105-369. The fact that property tax collection remedies are available for nuisance abatement costs and housing code enforcement costs does not subject those debts to all administrative provisions applicable to property taxes.

40. For more details on how bankruptcy law affects local tax collections, see *Fundamentals,* chapter 16.

pending. It applies to all debts, regardless of whether those debts arose before the bankruptcy petition was filed or after. Willful violations of the automatic stay can put a creditor at risk of court sanctions and fines. If a tax collector were to move forward with a foreclosure after learning that the taxpayer had filed for bankruptcy, that tax collector and that local government could be subject to sanctions.[41]

Most bankruptcies, especially Chapter 7 "liquidation" proceedings[42] that make up the bulk of bankruptcy filings, are resolved in only a few months. But some bankruptcies can continue for several years, including Chapter 13 "reorganization" bankruptcies[43] that may extend up to five years. Tax collectors may not start new collection efforts or continue existing collection efforts, including *in rem* foreclosures, until a bankruptcy proceeding ends in either a dismissal or a discharge.

A dismissal occurs when the debtor fails to comply with the court's requirements and the judge involuntarily terminates the debtor's bankruptcy proceeding. If a bankruptcy petition is dismissed, local tax collectors can proceed as if the bankruptcy proceeding never occurred. All taxes remain collectible as usual and all collection remedies can be employed as permitted by the Machinery Act.

A discharge occurs when the debtor satisfies all of the court's requirements and is granted relief from some (but not all) of her debts. Most local taxes will remain collectible, with the exception of personal property taxes that were not a lien on real property and that have been delinquent for more than one year. Often these are motor vehicle taxes levied prior to 2013's "Tag & Tax Together" system.[44]

Discharges do not affect property tax liens, however. These liens remain in place after a discharge and may be enforced using mortgage-style or *in rem* tax foreclosure procedures under the Machinery Act.[45] As a result, for taxes that are liens on real property, a bankruptcy filing might delay collection but should not prevent collection because foreclosure will still be an option after the bankruptcy proceeding ends.

The bottom line: once a bankruptcy proceeding ends in either a dismissal or a discharge, the tax office may move forward with a foreclosure against any property still owned by the taxpayer and subject to a lien for delinquent taxes.

---

41. A violation of the automatic stay must be willful to trigger court sanctions. 11 U.S.C. § 362(h). A collection action is considered willful only when that action was taken with knowledge of a bankruptcy filing by the debtor. *Id.* § 362.11. Often a tax collector will not learn of a bankruptcy filing until after she begins a foreclosure or other collection action. So long as the collector stops the foreclosure or other collection action immediately upon confirming with the court that the taxpayer has filed a bankruptcy petition, the collector will not be at risk of court sanctions.

42. Referencing Chapter 7 of the federal Bankruptcy Code, codified at Title 11 of the U.S. Code.

43. 11 U.S.C. Ch. 13.

44. For more details on the Tag & Tax Together system, see Chris McLaughlin, *County Tax Collection Obligations for Motor Vehicles Under the "Tag & Tax Together" Program*, COATES' CANONS: NC LOCAL GOV'T L. BLOG (UNC School of Government, Aug. 19, 2013), http://canons.sog.unc.edu/?p=7253.

45. The only time a bankruptcy proceeding should affect a tax lien on real property is when the bankruptcy court orders the property sold free and clear of all liens, with the liens to attach to the proceeds. This action is known as a "Section 363 sale." Creditors holding liens on the real property in question should receive advance notice and the opportunity to object to a Section 363 sale because if the sale occurs, foreclosure will no longer be an option to collect those liens. A tax collector may wish to object to the sale if the court plans to accept "credit" bids in which a creditor may buy the property in return for relinquishing a debt owed by the debtor. For example, a mortgage holder might buy the property in return for waiving the mortgage debt it holds on the property. Such a sale would not produce any funds to pay off the local tax liens on the property.

IV. The *In Rem* Checklist

Local governments using *in rem* foreclosure are wise to maintain detailed documentation of every step in the process. Doing so will help keep the effort organized, ensure that all statutory requirements are met, and provide a strong defense if the foreclosure is later challenged in court. Form 1, the *in rem* foreclosure checklist used by Orange County, on page 14, below, is an excellent example. The actions included on that checklist are described in detail in the sections below.

V. Advertising Tax Liens Prior to Initiating an *In Rem* Foreclosure

Local governments wishing to use the *in rem* foreclosure process must first advertise the tax liens that will be included in the foreclosures and then wait at least thirty days before starting the foreclosure process.[46] The Machinery Act requires that *all* liens on real property for delinquent taxes from the current year be advertised annually, of course.[47] But the only explicit penalty on local governments for failing to advertise is the elimination of the *in rem* foreclosure remedy.[48]

For a detailed discussion of the tax lien advertising process, local tax officials should refer to chapter 9 of the School of Government's *Fundamentals of Property Tax Collection Law in North Carolina*.[49] As a quick refresher, here are some of the most important points to remember about tax lien advertisements:

1. The advertisement should list the properties under the name of the record owners as of the delinquency date (January 6 of the current fiscal year) and/or the names of taxpayers who have become record owners since that date.[50]
2. The names of taxpayers with pending bankruptcy proceedings or pending appeals of their current year's tax assessments should not be advertised. These assessment appeals could be pending before the county board of equalization and review, the state Property Tax Commission, or state courts.[51] The *in rem* foreclosure process cannot be employed during a pending bankruptcy or tax appeal.[52]

---

46. G.S. 105-375(b).

47. G.S. 105-369.

48. Mortgage-style foreclosures under G.S. 105-374 are not dependent on prior tax lien advertisements. Nor are either of the collection remedies against personal property, levy and sale under G.S. 105-366 and -367 and attachment and garnishment under G.S. 105-368. And the advertising provision itself repeatedly states that failure to advertise correctly does not affect a local government's authority to collect the tax liens in question. G.S. 105-369(b1), (c), and (f).

49. See note 22, above, for a full citation.

50. G.S. 105-369(c)(1a).

51. The automatic stay that arises in federal bankruptcy proceedings prohibits any collection actions against the bankruptcy debtor. *See Fundamentals*, ch. 16. Similarly, G.S. 105-378 bars all enforced collection actions for taxes that are under appeal. Advertising tax liens could be construed as a collection action in both circumstances.

52. Tax collectors should not pursue *any* collection actions for any taxes for taxpayers in pending bankruptcies. But tax collectors may pursue collection actions, including *in rem* foreclosures, against taxpayers with pending tax appeals so long as those actions concern taxes from years that are not under appeal. For example, if Billy Blue Devil has a pending appeal for his 2015 tax assessment and delinquent taxes from 2014, the county could pursue an *in rem* foreclosure for the 2014 tax liens while the 2015 tax assessment appeal remains pending.

Form 1. *In Rem* Foreclosure Checklist

TAXPAYER NAME:		**PIN #:**	
TRACT:	**TAX MAP:**	**STREET ADDRESS:**	
STRUCTURES:		**VACANT:**	
COLLECTION ATTEMPTS: Garnishment/Attachment of Bank Accts or Rents/Levy on Personal Property			
RESEARCH: Internet Search: DMV Search: Field Visit:			
TELEPHONE CALLS MADE:			
TRANSFER LETTER: October	**DELINQUENT NOTICE:** January	**LIEN ADV. NOTICE:** G.S. 105-369(b)(1) February	**LIEN ADV.:** March
TITLE SEARCH: Work Completed: Updated:		**CERTIFIED MAIL:** G.S. 105-375(c)(1) (30 days before docketing judgment) Cost: $ Date:	
ADDITIONAL ATTEMPTS AT NOTICE: G.S. 105-375(c)(4)a First-Class Mail Sent:		**ADVERTISEMENT:** G.S. 105-375(c)(4)b. Dates Published: Newspaper: Cost: $	
JUDGMENT DOCKETED: G.S. 105-375(b) (at least 30 days after tax lien advertisement) Date: Cost: ($6.00 1st page and $0.25 each additional page)		**JUDGMENT MAILED TO TAXPAYER AND LIENHOLDERS:** First-Class Mail: (Not required by law)	
LETTER INFORMING TAXPAYER OF EXECUTION: (Two months after judgment filed) Date:		**REQUEST FOR EXECUTION G.S. 105-375(i):** (Three months after judgment) Date: (Execution fee $25.00 + $30.00 service fee)	

NOTICE OF SALE UNDER EXECUTION: G.S. 105-375(c) (30 days prior to sale/ Notify IRS at least 30 days prior to sale)			
CERTIFIED MAIL SENT:	Date:	Cost: $	
FIRST-CLASS MAIL SENT:	Date:		
NOTICE POSTED ON PROPERTY:	Date:		
NOTICE POSTED AT COURTHOUSE:	Date:		
PUBLICATION OF NOTICE OF SALE:	Dates:	Cost: $ Newspaper:	

(G.S. 1-339.52. The date of the first publication to the date of the last publication, both dates inclusive, shall not be less than 7 days, including Sundays; and the date of the last publication shall be not more than 10 days preceding the date of the sale.)			
SALE HELD:	**REPORT OF SALE:**	**UPSET BIDS:**	**ORDER OF CONFIRMATION:**
RETURN OF EXECUTION:		**NOTES:**	

3. The tax lien amounts should include all taxes that are a lien on the real property in question, including taxes on personal property (other than registered motor vehicles) listed by the same taxpayer in the jurisdiction for the same tax year.[53] Unlike taxpayer identification errors discussed below, tax amount errors in an advertisement probably do not warrant the publication of a corrected advertisement. The primary goal of the advertisement is to put the taxpayer on notice of the delinquent taxes and the possibility that the tax office might foreclose on the taxpayer's real property for those taxes. The fact that an advertisement contained the wrong amount of taxes owed by a taxpayer would almost certainly not affect the validity of a subsequent foreclosure, assuming that the tax office incorporated the correct amount of delinquent taxes, interests, and costs in the foreclosure.

4. If the tax office realizes that it failed to send the required notice to a taxpayer who is to be included in the advertisement, the tax office should send that notice immediately and either (i) delay publication of the full advertisement long enough to provide the omitted taxpayer a minimum of thirty days prior publication or (ii) remove the omitted taxpayer from the full advertisement and publish a separate, individual advertisement for the omitted taxpayer no earlier than thirty days after notice is sent.[54] Similarly, if the tax office realizes after the advertisement is published that a taxpayer was omitted from that advertisement, the tax office should run a separate, individual advertisement for the omitted taxpayer.[55] Failure to advertise a taxpayer could jeopardize the validity of a subsequent foreclosure against the omitted taxpayer.

5. The local government may not docket a foreclosure judgment until at least thirty days after the tax liens were advertised.

VI. The Title Search and Notice of Foreclosure to Interested Parties

Failure to provide adequate notice to all parties who might have an interest in the property being sold is the one error that is most likely to jeopardize the validity of a foreclosure. This is especially true when a local government relies on the expedited *in rem* method of foreclosure, which lacks some of the safeguards inherent in the civil action required of a mortgage-style foreclosure.

Notice must be given at least thirty days prior to the docketing of the foreclosure judgment.[56] As mentioned above, there is also a minimum thirty-day waiting period between advertising the tax liens and docketing the judgment. Theoretically, the local government could send the foreclosure notice on the same day it publishes its tax lien advertisement and then docket the judgment thirty days later. But in practice, most local governments will first advertise the tax liens in the hope that that publicity will encourage the taxpayer to pay the delinquent taxes and avoid foreclosure. Then

---

53. G.S. 105-355(a).

54. G.S. 105-369(b1) requires that taxpayers receive notice of the intent to advertise at least thirty days before the advertisement is published. The cost of this advertisement should be allocated in equal shares to all taxpayers included in the advertisement. That cost can and should be recovered along with principal taxes and interest in a foreclosure.

55. This obligation to give proper notice and to include the taxpayer in the advertisement is important only if the tax office plans to pursue *in rem* foreclosure against the omitted taxpayer. If not, then the advertising error likely has no legal repercussions for the tax office, and it may not be worth the money and time to correct the error.

56. G.S. 105-375(c)(1).

the local government will begin the title search necessary to identify any parties in addition to the taxpayer who must receive notice of the foreclosure.

The tax office must give notice to the owner of the property and to "all lienholders of record who have a lien against the taxpayer (including any liens referred to in the conveyance of the property to the taxpayer)."[57] The process of identifying these parties is known as a title search and can involve many hours of work.

Title searches and the law that governs real property ownership can be complex. A full exploration of the process is beyond the scope of this publication. Tax officials who will be involved in title searches should receive training from legal professionals with experience in this area of law. A good starting point is the *Collection Procedures Manual* maintained by the North Carolina Tax Collectors' Association.[58]

With those recommendations in mind, here is a brief overview of a title search. The goal is to identify every party that might have an interest in the subject property as of the date of the foreclosure notice. To do this, the tax office will need to create a "chain of title" that documents the ownership history of the property. This history should include all parties that have owned or currently own the property or that have some type of interest in the property. Interests in property come in many forms, including

1. fee simple ("regular" ownership);
2. tenancy by the entirety (spousal ownership);
3. life tenancy and remaindermen;
4. deeds of trust and similar mortgage liens;
5. local, state, and federal tax liens;
6. judgment liens (held by parties that have successfully sued the owner of the property);
7. Medicaid and Medicare liens;
8. Uniform Commercial Code security interests;
9. easements;
10. government condemnations and rights of way (usually for highways, railroads, and utilities);
11. leases; and
12. lis pendens (notice of a pending lawsuit involving the property).

Any party that holds any of these property interests must receive notice of the pending *in rem* foreclosure against the property.[59] If the tax office thinks a party might have an ownership interest in the property but is not certain, the tax office should err on the side of inclusion and provide that party with notice.

The tax office must be certain to obtain the correct names and addresses of the current owners of all interests in the property. If the property has been transferred since it was last listed for taxation, the tax office must send notice of the foreclosure to the current owner and not the listing owner.

---

57. *Id.*

58. Available on the North Carolina Tax Collectors' Association website, www.nctca.org/sites/default/files/content/docs/CollectionProceeduresManual.pdf (last visited May 21, 2015).

59. Some of these property interests may not be affected by a tax foreclosure. For example, easements that existed before the first tax lien included in the foreclosure will not be affected by the foreclosure. *See* Chris McLaughlin, *Taxes, Telephones and Traffic Cones: Do Tax Foreclosures Extinguish Easements?* Coates' Canons: NC Local Gov't L. Blog (UNC School of Government, Sept. 3, 2009), http://canons.sog.unc.edu/?p=557. Regardless, the tax office should still give notice of the foreclosure to all interested parties even if it is not clear that their interests will be affected.

The same is true for changes in deeds of trust and all other interests in the property; notice must be sent to the current holder of that interest, which may be different from the party that held that interest when the property was listed for taxation.

The two main sources of documents in a title search will be the register of deeds and the clerk of superior court. The register of deeds is the repository of most real property records, including deeds, mortgages, leases, easements, and rights of way. Tax office staff will need to research all transfers to and from all grantors (the party who is conveying an interest) and grantees (the party receiving an interest) in the property's chain of title. The clerk of superior court will have records concerning judgments, civil actions, special proceedings, and partition proceedings. Tax office staff must search for any court filings relating to any of the property's current and prior owners that might affect their interests in the property or give other parties interests in the property.

Neither the Machinery Act nor any other state law provision offers any guidance on perhaps the most important question concerning the pre-foreclosure title search: How many years into the past must the search extend? Experienced property tax professionals recommend looking back at least thirty years. UNC School of Government faculty member Charles Szypszak, an expert in real property law, reports that thirty-five years is the common title search period employed by attorneys who specialize in real property conveyances.[60]

There is no magic number of years that will render a title search and a foreclosure immune from challenges. The tax office simply needs to be able to demonstrate that it employed due diligence in identifying all interested parties in case the foreclosure is later challenged by a party who claims an interest in the property and who did not receive notice. Thirty or thirty-five years for a title search seems to be a reasonable compromise between the tax office's budget and staff constraints and its desire for a complete and accurate chain of title.

Once the parties are identified, notice must be mailed via registered or certified mail, return receipt requested.[61] All mail receipts should be retained by the tax office as proof of notice should a party object to the foreclosure based on lack of notice.

A. Special Concern for Military Members

The federal Servicemembers Civil Relief Act (SCRA)[62] prohibits tax collectors from selling real property owned by active duty military personnel unless a court determines that the taxpayer's military service did not materially affect his or her ability to pay the delinquent taxes.

To avoid SCRA concerns, after identifying all parties with an interest in the property the tax office must make an effort to determine if any of those parties are actively serving in the United States military. Outside of information provided directly by the military member, the most accurate source for military service information is the SCRA website maintained by the United States Department of Defense.[63]

After investigating the military statuses of all interested parties, the tax office should file an affidavit with the court indicating each party's status. In the case of unknown heirs or owners (a situation which often arises in connection with estate property formerly owned by a deceased taxpayer), the

---

60. Charles Szypszak, *Public Registries and Private Solutions: An Evolving American Real Estate Conveyance Regime,* 24 WHITTIER L. REV. 663, 682–93 (2002–2003) (describing the standard thirty-five-year title search and how title insurance will usually cover older title concerns).
61. G.S. 105-375(c)(3).
62. 50 U.S.C. app. §§ 501–597.
63. *See* https://www.dmdc.osd.mil/appj/scra/scraHome.do.

Form 2. Servicemembers Civil Relief Act Affidavit

STATE OF NORTH CAROLINA	File No.
_____ County	In The General Court Of Justice

Name And Address Of Plaintiff	
VERSUS	**SERVICEMEMBERS CIVIL RELIEF ACT AFFIDAVIT**
Name And Address Of Defendant	50 U.S.C. 3901 to 4043

NOTE: *This form is not for use in Chapter 45 Foreclosure actions.*

AFFIDAVIT

I, the undersigned Affiant, under penalty of perjury declare the following to be true:

1. As of the current date: *(check one of the following)*
   - [ ] a. the defendant named above is in military service.*
   - [ ] b. the defendant named above is **not** in military service.*
   - [ ] c. I am unable to determine whether the defendant named above is in military service.*

2. *(check one or more of the following)*
   - [ ] a. I [ ] have [ ] have not used the Servicemembers Civil Relief Act Website (https://www.dmdc.osd.mil/appj/scra/) to determine the defendant's military status. [ ] The results from my use of that website are attached.
     (**NOTE:** *The Servicemembers Civil Relief Act Website is a website maintained by the Department of Defense (DoD). If DoD security certificates are not installed on your computer, you may experience security alerts from your internet browser when you attempt to access the website. DoD security certificates were automatically added to the computers of all Judicial Branch users, such that these users should not expect security alerts to appear with this website after July of 2015. As of December 14, 2015, the Servicemembers Civil Relief Act Website includes the following advice: "Most web browsers don't come with the DoD certificates already installed. The best and most secure solution is for the user to install all of the DoD's public certificates in their web browser.")*
   - [ ] b. The following facts support my statement as to the defendant's military service: *(State how you know the defendant is not in the military. Be specific.)*

     _____
     _____
     _____
     _____
     _____

*NOTE: *The term "military service" includes the following: active duty service as a member of the United States Army, Navy, Air Force, Marine Corps, or Coast Guard; service as a member of the National Guard under a call to active service authorized by the President or the Secretary of Defense for a period of more than 30 consecutive days for purposes of responding to a national emergency; active service as a commissioned officer of the Public Health Service or of the National Oceanic and Atmospheric Administration; any period of service during which a servicemember is absent from duty on account of sickness, wounds, leave, or other lawful cause. 50 U.S.C. 3911(2).*

SWORN/AFFIRMED AND SUBSCRIBED TO BEFORE ME	Date
Date	Signature Of Affiant
Signature Of Person Authorized To Administer Oaths	Name Of Affiant (type or print)

[ ] Deputy CSC [ ] Assistant CSC [ ] Clerk Of Superior Court [ ] Magistrate

SEAL [ ] Notary | Date My Commission Expires

NOTE TO COURT: *Do not proceed to enter judgment in a non-criminal case in which the defendant has not made an appearance until a Servicemembers Civil Relief Act affidavit (whether on this form or not) has been filed, and if it appears that the defendant is in military service, do not proceed to enter judgment until such time that you have appointed an attorney to represent him or her.*

(Over)

AOC-G-250, Rev. 12/15
© 2015 Administrative Office of the Courts

Information About Servicemembers Civil Relief Act Affidavits

1. **Plaintiff to file affidavit**
   In any civil action or proceeding, including any child custody proceeding, in which the defendant does not make an appearance, the court, before entering judgment for the plaintiff, shall require the plaintiff to file with the court an affidavit—
   - (A) stating whether or not the defendant is in military service and showing necessary facts to support the affidavit; or
   - (B) if the plaintiff is unable to determine whether or not the defendant is in military service, stating that the plaintiff is unable to determine whether or not the defendant is in military service.
   50 U.S.C. 3931(b)(1).

2. **Appointment of attorney to represent defendant in military service**
   If in a civil action or proceeding in which the defendant does not make an appearance it appears that the defendant is in military service, the court may not enter a judgment until after the court appoints an attorney to represent the defendant. If an attorney appointed to represent a service member cannot locate the service member, actions by the attorney in the case shall not waive any defense of the service member or otherwise bind the service member. 50 U.S.C. 3931(b)(2). State funds are not available to pay attorneys appointed pursuant to the Servicemembers Civil Relief Act. To comply with the federal Violence Against Women Act and in consideration of G.S. 50B-2(a), 50C-2(b), and 50D-2(b), plaintiffs in Chapter 50B, Chapter 50C, and Chapter 50D proceedings should not be required to pay the costs of attorneys appointed pursuant to the Servicemembers Civil Relief Act. Plaintiffs in other types of actions and proceedings may be required to pay the costs of attorneys appointed pursuant to the Servicemembers Civil Relief Act. The allowance or disallowance of the ordering of costs will require a case-specific analysis.

3. **Defendant's military status not ascertained by affidavit**
   If based upon the affidavits filed in such an action, the court is unable to determine whether the defendant is in military service, the court, before entering judgment, may require the plaintiff to file a bond in an amount approved by the court. If the defendant is later found to be in military service, the bond shall be available to indemnify the defendant against any loss or damage the defendant may suffer by reason of any judgment for the plaintiff against the defendant, should the judgment be set aside in whole or in part. The bond shall remain in effect until expiration of the time for appeal and setting aside of a judgment under applicable Federal or State law or regulation or under any applicable ordinance of a political subdivision of a State. The court may issue such orders or enter such judgments as the court determines necessary to protect the rights of the defendant under this Act. 50 U.S.C. 3931(b)(3).

4. **Satisfaction of requirement for affidavit**
   The requirement for an affidavit above may be satisfied by a statement, declaration, verification, or certificate, in writing, subscribed and certified or declared to be true under penalty of perjury. 50 U.S.C. 3931(b)(4). The presiding judicial official will determine whether the submitted affidavit is sufficient.

5. **Penalty for making or using false affidavit**
   A person who makes or uses an affidavit permitted under 50 U.S.C. 3931(b) (or a statement, declaration, verification, or certificate as authorized under 50 U.S.C. 3931(b)(4)) knowing it to be false, shall be fined as provided in title 18, United States Code, or imprisoned for not more than one year, or both. 50 U.S.C. 3931(c).

AOC-G-250, Side Two, Rev. 12/15
© 2015 Administrative Office of the Courts

tax office must indicate that it has been unable to confirm the military status of all interested parties. See Form 2, on pages 18–19, above. Some courts require their own affidavit forms.[64]

If a local government determines that an owner is active duty military, the best approach may be to put the foreclosure on hold. Even if a court were to determine that the foreclosure may proceed because the party's military service did not affect the taxpayer's ability to pay the taxes in question, the military member would possess the right to redeem the property—in other words, reverse the foreclosure sale—up to 180 days after the sale. That right of redemption must be disclosed at the foreclosure sale and could scare away all potential bidders.

Waiting on a foreclosure proceeding until after the owner leaves active duty military service should not raise statute of limitation concerns. The period during which a taxpayer is serving in the military does not count toward the Machinery Act's ten-year statute of limitations on enforced collections.[65]

B. Contents and Mailing of Notice

The notice should identify the property being foreclosed upon; state the amount of taxes, interest, costs, and penalties that must be paid to satisfy the delinquent tax liens; and inform the recipient that the foreclosure will be terminated if the taxes and related amounts are paid in full. The costs should include the costs of serving the notice and the estimated cost of publishing notice of the foreclosure in the newspaper. As discussed in detail below, the amount owed on the property should include Machinery Act interest up to the date of the notice and the $250 administrative fee authorized by the *in rem* provisions.[66] The notice should also indicate that additional amounts may accrue on the property if the foreclosure proceeds. Forms 3 and 4, on pages 21 and 22, respectively, are examples of notice letters for owners and lienholders, respectively.

The notices should be sent via certified mail, return receipt requested, as well as by first-class mail. For recordkeeping purposes, the local government should keep all return receipts for all notices sent during the *in rem* process. When the tax collector later dockets the judgment, the collector should file those return receipts along with a copy of the notice and a "certificate of service" confirming that the notices were mailed to the taxpayer and advertised at least thirty days prior to the docketing of the judgment. See Form 5, on page 23, below.

C. Estate Property and Unknown Owners

In many cases, the title search may demonstrate that one or more unknown parties have interests in the property. Usually this occurs with "estate property," where the property owner has died but where there has been no probate proceeding to determine to whom ownership of the property has been transferred.

Unless and until a court probates a will or applies intestacy law to the estate property, record ownership of the property should remain in the name of "Estate of Jane Doe" or "Heirs of Jane Doe." If the tax office learns of an estate administrator, then notice should be provided to that party. But often there will be no additional information about the estate other than documentation of the owner's death. In that case, the tax office should identify all possible heirs of the owner (spouses, children,

---

64. For example, see Wake County Superior Court's affidavit here: www.nccourts.org/county/wake/Documents/Affidavit-re-Servicemembers-Civil-Relief-Act.pdf.

65. 50 U.S.C. app. § 206.

66. G.S. 105-375(c)(5).

Form 3. Notice Letter to Owner via Certified Mail, Return Receipt Requested, and via First-Class Mail

Dear _____:

    The records of _____ County show that you are the owner of the real property described below. Property taxes assessed against the property by _____ County [and the municipality of _____] for the years _____ are past due and remain unpaid. These taxes, together with penalties, interest, and costs, constitute a first lien upon the property.

    Unless the amount shown below is paid to the county within thirty days from this date, or a satisfactory arrangement for payment is made, it will be my duty to docket a judgment against the property in the Office of the Clerk of Superior Court of _____ County. The judgment will be executed in the manner provided by law, and the property will be sold at public sale to the highest bidder.

Amount of tax: $ _____

Penalties and interest: $ _____

Costs: $ _____

Total due: $ _____

Property: [Enter here a description sufficient to identify the property, including address and PIN*].

_____

_____

    If the judgment is docketed or execution is placed in the hands of the sheriff, additional costs will accrue. I trust that you will pay the amount due promptly and avoid either added expense to you or the loss of your property.

    Very truly yours,

_____

Tax Collector

*PIN = a property identification number assigned by the county tax office.

---

siblings, etc.) and send them individual notice. Other unknown owners should be given notice through a posting placed on the property and via advertising of the foreclosure in a local newspaper.[67]

D. Posting and Advertising the Foreclosure

The *in rem* provision requires posting notice of the foreclosure "in a conspicuous place on the property" only if service by mail on interested parties is unsuccessful.[68] That said, best practice is for the collector to *always* post notice of the foreclosure on the property. Doing so will provide

---

67. Although the *in rem* provision requires advertisement in a newspaper with general circulation in the county where the property lies, in the case of estate property it might be wise to also advertise in a newspaper published in the county where the deceased owner last resided if that was a different county.

68. G.S. 105-375(c)(4)(a).

Form 4. Initial Notice Letter to Lienholder via Certified Mail, Return Receipt Requested, and via First-Class Mail

Dear _____:

The records of _____ County show that you have a lien against the property described below, which is currently owned by _____. Taxes assessed against the property by _____ County [and the municipality of _____] for the years _____ are past due and remain unpaid. These taxes, together with penalties, interest, and costs, constitute a first lien upon the property.

Unless the amount shown below is paid to the county within thirty days from this date, or a satisfactory arrangement for payment is made, it will be my duty to docket a judgment against the property in the Office of the Clerk of Superior Court of _____ County. The judgment will be executed in the manner provided by law, and the property will be sold at public sale to the highest bidder. **If the property is sold, it will be sold free and clear of your lien.**

Amount of tax: $ _____

Penalties and interest: $ _____

Costs: $ _____

Total due: $ _____

Property: [Enter here a description sufficient to identify the property including address and PIN*].

_____

_____

If the judgment is docketed or execution is placed in the hands of the sheriff, additional costs will accrue. I trust that you will pay the amount due promptly and avoid either added expense to you or the loss of your lien on the property.

Very truly yours,

_____

Tax Collector

*PIN = a property identification number assigned by the county tax office.

Form 5. Certificate of Service

STATE OF NORTH CAROLINA

COUNTY OF _____

IN THE GENERAL COURT OF JUSTICE

DISTRICT COURT DIVISION

FILE NO. _____ M _____

_____

Plaintiff

vs.   CERTIFICATE OF SERVICE

_____

Defendant(s)

I hereby certify that copies of the letter attached as Exhibit A were sent to the defendants by certified mail, return receipt requested, and by first-class mail; a copy of the related return receipts are attached as Exhibit B. In accordance with G.S. 105-375(c), notice was published on _____ and _____ [dates of advertisements] in the _____ [newspaper] and was posted on the property described in the notice on _____ [date notice was posted on property]. A copy of said notice is attached hereto as Exhibit C.

This the _____ day of _____, 20____.

_____

Tax Collector, _____ County

additional evidence of the collector's efforts to notify interested parties (especially unknown owners, as mentioned above) and, perhaps more importantly, might attract more bidders to the upcoming foreclosure sale.

Publishing notice of the foreclosure in the local newspaper is another opportunity to demonstrate the tax office's due diligence to provide notice to all interested parties. As with posting on the property, the Machinery Act requires publication only when service by mail fails.[69] But again, best practice is for collectors to *always* advertise foreclosures in the local newspaper (especially when unknown owners exist).

The advertisements must be published in a newspaper of "general circulation in the county" at least once a week for two consecutive weeks. To meet this standard, a newspaper must have a reasonable number of subscribers who are located throughout the county and not limited to one particular area.[70]

Form 6, on page 24, below, provides an example of the type of notice that should be published. The local government should keep copies of the actual newspapers in which the notices are published as proof of the additional efforts it has taken to provide notice of the foreclosure to all interested parties. It is also good practice for the tax collector to file with the court an affidavit certifying publication and to attach to the affidavit a copy of the advertisement. This effort will help minimize title concerns down the road.

---

69. G.S. 105-375(c)(4)(b).

70. For more details on the choice of newspaper, see *Fundamentals*, chapter 9.

Form 6. Publication Notice of *In Rem* Foreclosure

STATE OF NORTH CAROLINA

COUNTY OF _____

FILE NO. _____

IN THE GENERAL COURT OF JUSTICE

_____ COURT DIVISION

_____
            Plaintiff

vs.   NOTICE

_____
            Defendant(s)

Pursuant to the requirements of G.S. 105-375(c), notice is hereby given to

_____ (Current owners)

_____

_____ (Lienholders)

_____

that a judgment of foreclosure will be docketed against the property described below on

_____

[Here enter a brief description of the property.]

Execution will be issued on the judgment, and the property will be sold as provided by law. The tax lien, including interests and costs, may be paid before the judgment is docketed and at any time thereafter as allowed by law.

_____   _____
(Name of newspaper and dates notice is to be published)   Tax Collector

                                                    _____
                                                    Date notice prepared

VII. Docketing the Judgment

At least thirty days after providing notice to all interested parties, the tax collector is authorized to file with the clerk of superior court a certificate indicating the amounts owed on the property being foreclosed upon.[71]

When filing this certificate, the local government should request that the clerk assign it an "M" designation (for "miscellaneous") rather than a "CVD" (for "civil district" court) or a "CVS" ("civil superior" court) designation. Filing fees are $6 for the first page, and 25 cents per additional page.[72] Many courts allow local governments pursuing tax foreclosures to wait to pay the filing fee until either the taxes are paid or the property is sold, whichever comes first, as permitted by G.S. 105-375(b).

As mentioned above, when the judgment is docketed the tax collector should also file a "certificate of service" documenting the efforts to notify all interested parties of the foreclosure action. See Form 5, on page 23, above.

The certificate docketed by the local government will serve as a judgment against the property and allow the local government to "execute" on that judgment by selling the property. The certificate must include

1. the name(s) of listing taxpayer(s) of the property;
2. a description of the property "sufficient to permit its identification"; and
3. the amount of taxes, penalties, interests, and costs that are liens on the property along with the tax years for which these amounts are due.

See Form 7, on page 26, below for an example of what the judgment should include.
Details about each of these requirements are set out in the sections below.

A. Taxpayer Names

The *in rem* statute requires that the certificate be in the name of the "taxpayer" as defined by G.S. 105-273(17): "A person whose property is subject to ad valorem property taxation by any county or municipality and any person who . . . has a duty to list property for taxation." It follows that the name included on the certificate should be the listing taxpayer(s) for the most recent year of taxation. That owner may not be the current owner if the property has been sold since it was last listed for taxation. However, as discussed extensively above, the local government should make sure it provides notice to all current owners, even if their names are not included in the certificate that is docketed with the court.

B. Property Description

The certificate should include the full legal description of the property from the most recent deed and a recording reference to that deed so that an interested observer could locate the deed in question. An address and county tax office "PIN" (property identification number) should also be included on the certificate.

---

71. G.S. 105-375(b).
72. G.S. 7A-308(a)(11).

Form 7. Judgment for Taxes Owed

STATE OF NORTH CAROLINA

COUNTY OF _____

FILE NO. _____

IN THE GENERAL COURT OF JUSTICE

_____ COURT DIVISION

BEFORE THE CLERK

_____
            Plaintiff

vs.   JUDGMENT FOR TAXES

_____
            Defendant(s)
[Name of current owners and lienholders]

Pursuant to the provisions of Section 105-375 of the General Statutes, I hereby certify that taxes duly levied and assessed by _____ County [City, Town] for the years _____ against the property described below are due and unpaid; that these taxes constitute a first lien upon the real property hereinafter described prior to any other lien that is or may become attached to the real property; that the amount now owing to _____ County [City, Town] on account of the taxes, penalties, interest, and costs is as follows:

Amount of tax for _____ $_____

Penalties $_____

Costs of advertising $_____

Subtotal $_____

Interest on the subtotal from _____ to date $_____

Administrative charge $_____250.00___

Mailing and publication costs $_____

Total amount of judgment $_____

That _____ County [City, Town] has a first lien for the amount of the judgment, plus interest at the rate of 8 percent per annum from date until paid, upon the following described real estate located in _____ Township, _____ County, North Carolina:

_____

[Insert full legal description, deed reference, and PIN*].

This _____ day of_____, _____.

Filed _____
Docketed _____, at _____ ___.M.

_____
Clerk of the Superior Court

_____
Tax Collector for [City] [Town]

[County] of _____

*PIN = a property identification number assigned by the county tax office.

C. Taxes, Penalties, Costs, and Interest

The sections below describe how these line items should be handled.

1. Taxes

All unpaid taxes that are a lien on the property and can be accurately determined at the time the certificate is docketed should be included in the certificate so that they can be collected in the fore-closure sale. This total should include taxes that are more than ten years past due and taxes that are not yet delinquent.

With respect to old taxes, the Machinery Act creates a ten-year statute of limitation on the use of enforced collection remedies.[73] However, statutes of limitation are "affirmative defenses" that must be raised by the taxpayer in order to limit a local government's actions.[74] If a taxpayer fails to object to the inclusion of taxes that are more than ten years past due, then the foreclosure action is effective for all taxes included in the judgment.[75] With that caveat in mind, the local government should include all delinquent taxes in the judgment regardless of year and put the burden of enforcing the statute of limitations on the delinquent taxpayer.

With respect to new taxes that are not yet delinquent, the *in rem* provision does not require that the taxes included in the judgment be delinquent, only that they already be a lien on the property.[76]

For example, assume Carolina County is pursuing an *in rem* foreclosure against Wanda Wolfpack's property at 123 Main Street. Wanda owes 2013 and 2014 delinquent taxes on the property. The *in rem* certificate is prepared for docketing on July 15, 2015. As of that date, the county has assigned a tax value for 2015 to 123 Main Street and has adopted its 2015–2016 tax rate. The tax office should include the 2015 taxes on 123 Main Street in the *in rem* certificate because they are a lien on the property (as of January 1, 2015) and they are able to be calculated as of the date of the certificate. These taxes should be included in the *in rem* foreclosure despite the fact that they are not yet delinquent. At the foreclosure sale, the property will be sold free and clear of the 2015 tax lien because those taxes were included in the foreclosure certificate.

Assume similar facts but that the *in rem* certificate for Wanda's property is prepared on May 15, 2015, at which time the county has yet to set its tax rate for the 2015–2016 tax year. Then the 2015 taxes on 123 Main Street should not be included in the *in rem* certificate because they cannot be calculated accurately at the time the certificate is docketed. At the foreclosure sale, the property will be sold subject to the lien for 2015 property taxes—a fact that must be disclosed to all potential buy-ers of the property.

2. Other Debts That May Be Collected as Property Taxes

Any debts owed to a local government that create liens on real property should be included in the amounts owed. These debts include special assessments, nuisance abatement costs, minimum hous-ing code enforcement costs, ambulance service fees, and possibly solid waste fees.[77]

---

73. G.S. 105-378(a). This limitation runs from the original due date for the taxes in question, which for all property taxes other than taxes on registered motor vehicles is September 1 of the fiscal year for which the taxes were levied.

74. N.C. Rule of Civil Procedure 8(c) (G.S. 1A-1, Rule 8(c)).

75. Iredell Cty. v. Crawford, 262 N.C. 720 (1964) (if taxpayer fails to raise statute of limitations in his initial response to the foreclosure action, the local government may proceed with foreclosure regardless of the age of the taxes included).

76. G.S. 105-375(b).

77. See section II, question 7, above.

3. Administrative Costs

Most local governments will pursue *in rem* foreclosures without retaining attorneys, meaning attorneys' fees are usually not an issue in an *in rem* foreclosure. But as discussed above, the necessary title work will require a substantial investment of staff time. The Machinery Act recognizes the cost associated with that work, at least to some extent. G.S. 105-375(c)(5) authorizes the tax office to charge the taxpayer an "administrative" fee of $250 for their pre-foreclosure work.[78]

The $250 administrative fee is the maximum fee that the local tax office may charge a taxpayer for an *in rem* foreclosure, even if the local government incurs attorneys' fees as part of the process. The Machinery Act is clear that attorneys' fees may be charged to a taxpayer only after a complaint has been filed in a "mortgage-style" foreclosure. G.S. 105-374(i). In other words, no attorneys' fees may be charged to a taxpayer in an *in rem* foreclosure.

The tax office may not charge the administrative fee to the taxpayer unless and until it sends a foreclosure notice to the taxpayer.[79] This restriction remains effective regardless of how much time and money the tax office has spent preparing for the *in rem* foreclosure. If the taxpayer wishes to satisfy all outstanding taxes, interest, and costs on her property prior to the mailing of the foreclosure notice, the tax office may not require her to pay any administrative or legal fees relating to the pre-foreclosure work by tax office staff.

For example, assume Billy Blue Devil owes delinquent taxes and interest on his property in Carolina County. After advertising Billy's tax lien, the county conducts a thorough title search of Billy's property to determine all parties that might have an interest in that property. One day before the county plans to mail the required foreclosure notices to all interested parties, Billy appears at the tax office offering payment to stop the foreclosure. Despite the many hours of staff time already invested in the *in rem* foreclosure process, the tax office may not charge Billy any administrative fees or legal costs. If Billy pays the principal taxes, interest accrued to that date, and any other costs permitted by the Machinery Act (such as advertising costs), the county must accept payment and terminate the *in rem* foreclosure process for his property.

As discussed above, the required pre-foreclosure notice should include the $250 administrative fee. In the example above, if Billy appears at the tax office to pay his delinquent taxes at any point after the county has mailed the required foreclosure notices, the tax office may and should charge Billy the $250 administrative fee.[80]

4. Other Costs and Penalties

The foreclosure should include all costs and penalties that the Machinery Act authorizes to be charged to the taxpayer. These costs may be ones that arose prior to the *in rem* process (such as tax lien advertisement costs,[81] bad check penalties,[82] notice fees for attachments and garnishments[83]) and those

---

78. The *in rem* administrative fee was increased from $50 to $250 in 2011. *See* S.L. 2011-352. The increase was effective for all *in rem* foreclosures initiated on or after July 1, 2011.

79. As discussed above, the foreclosure notice must be sent to the taxpayer no earlier than thirty days prior to the date on which the local government dockets the foreclosure judgment. G.S. 105-374(c)(1).

80. The tax office should charge the taxpayer the $250 administrative fee even if the taxpayer has yet to receive the foreclosure notice. The administrative charge is validly levied on the date the tax office sends the foreclosure notice, not on the date the taxpayer receives the notice.

81. G.S. 105-369(d).

82. G.S. 105-357(b)(2).

83. G.S. 105-368(g).

associated with the *in rem* foreclosure itself (costs of mailing and publishing notice[84] and court fees for docketing the judgment[85]).

5. Interest

The Machinery Act requires that interest accrue on delinquent taxes and all related costs (advertising, bad check fees, etc.) from the delinquency date (January 6 of the fiscal year for which the tax was levied) at a rate of 2 percent for the first month and 0.75 percent for every subsequent month. G.S. 105-360. Interest generally continues until all of the principal taxes and costs have been paid.

In a foreclosure, the local government must provide to the court a final accounting of taxes and costs owed by the taxpayer well before those taxes and costs are paid by the sale proceeds. In a mortgage-style foreclosure, this accounting occurs when the attorney files the required certificate of taxes owed. G.S. 105-374(e). In an *in rem* foreclosure, this accounting occurs when the judgment is docketed. G.S. 105-375(b). Each type of accounting should include Machinery Act interest accrued to the date the accounting is filed or docketed.

It might be months or years from that date until a foreclosure sale is confirmed and the local government actually receives payment. Should interest continue to accrue on the delinquent amounts during that period?

The Machinery Act does not directly answer this question for mortgage-style foreclosures under G.S. 105-374. But for *in rem* foreclosures, the Machinery Act requires that the taxes, costs, penalties, and interest owed on the property begin to accrue 8 percent "post-judgment" interest after the judgment is docketed.[86] "Regular" Machinery Act interest should no longer accrue once the judgment is docketed. Unlike Machinery Act interest, post-judgment interest should be calculated on a per-diem (per-day) basis, meaning post-judgment interest accrues daily. The local government should collect the post-judgment interest from the sale proceeds along with taxes, Machinery Act interest, fees, and costs.

Here is an example of post-judgment interest calculation. Assume that Tina Tar Heel owes delinquent 2013 property taxes on her home in Carolina County. The county proceeds with *in rem* foreclosure against Tina's house and dockets its judgment on May 1, 2015, for a total of $5,000 in taxes, costs, and Machinery Act interest up to that date. Because the county has not yet finalized its tax rate for the fiscal year that opens on July 1, 2015, the county does not include the taxes for the 2015 fiscal year in the foreclosure.

The foreclosure sale is finalized on September 1, 2015, for a final bid of $10,000. The county should then accrue 121 days (May 1 to September 1) of 8 percent per annum post-judgment interest, which works out to $132 in additional interest. The county would collect this additional interest from the sale proceeds prior to paying the other taxes and costs owed on the property. The property would be sold subject to the lien for the 2015 taxes because those taxes were not included in the foreclosure.

Even if the foreclosure sale failed to produce enough funds to satisfy the post-judgment interest and the other amounts owed by the taxpayer, the property would still be sold free and clear of all liens for those debts. See section XV, below, for more details on post-sale procedures.

---

84. G.S. 105-375(c)(5).

85. G.S. 105-375(b). The statute suggests that the clerk of court should not require payment of these filing fees until the taxes are paid or the property is sold. That said, not all clerks of court will follow this mandate. If a clerk of court requires payment of these fees at the time of docketing, the tax office should pay them and later collect reimbursement from the taxpayer (if the taxpayer stops the foreclosure by paying all amounts owed on the property) or from the sale proceeds.

86. G.S. 105-375(d).

VIII. Appeals

The *in rem* foreclosure provisions do not reference any right of appeal for property owners or other parties with interests in the property being foreclosed upon. Experienced *in rem* practitioners across the state cannot recall any instance of an *in rem* judgment being appealed. That said, it seems that an appeal of a tax foreclosure is possible because the "regular" rules of civil procedure apply to these proceedings just as they apply to other types of civil actions.

G.S. 1-301.1, one of many provisions concerning civil appeals, creates a ten-day deadline for any "party aggrieved by an order or judgment entered by the clerk" to appeal. Rule 62 of the North Carolina Rules of Civil Procedure[87] creates a "stay" whenever a judgment is appealed. During this stay no execution on the appealed judgment may be issued, and without an execution of an *in rem* judgment the foreclosing government may not sell the property that is the subject of the judgment. But G.S. 1-292 requires the appellant (the party who is appealing the judgment) to post a bond in order for a judgment ordering the sale of property to be stayed during appeal.

Reading all of these provisions together, it appears that any party with an interest in the property being foreclosed upon has ten days from the date the *in rem* judgment is docketed to appeal. If the appealing party provides a bond to cover any loss of value in the property, then the judgment is stayed and the foreclosing government may not obtain an execution and sell the property until the appeal is resolved.

Resolution of an *in rem* appeal should be quick. G.S. 1-301.1 states that a judge may review the matter but can send it to the clerk of superior court for review if the matter in question is one delegated to the clerk. That seems to be the case with an *in rem* foreclosure, meaning that there should be no need or opportunity for full judicial review of the foreclosure action. The clerk should simply review the filings to make sure that the correct documents are in the record and that the correct parties received notice. If so, then the clerk should affirm the judgment, terminate the stay, and permit the local government to move for execution and sale of the property.

IX. Executing the Judgment

Between three months and two years after docketing its judgment, the tax office may ask the court to issue an "execution" on that judgment.[88] Execution allows the local government to enforce its judgment via a sale of the property that was the target of the foreclosure. As discussed in section II, question 7, above, local governments may combine separate judgments against one property for multiple local tax liens into one execution and sale. An execution is valid for only ninety days, meaning that the first notice of a foreclosure sale must occur within ninety days of the date the court issues the execution.[89]

Form 8 is a sample request for execution. Form 9, on page 32, below, is a sample of the execution order issued by the court directing the sheriff to sell the property being foreclosed upon. The bottom of Form 8 serves as the "return of execution" that the sheriff must complete after selling the property in question.

---

87. G.S. 1A-1, Rule 62.
88. G.S. 105-375(i).
89. G.S. 1-339.48 and 1-310. These provisions are satisfied so long as the sale is "commenced" by the publishing of the first notice of sale. Once that occurs, the actual sale can take place more than ninety days after the execution was issued without violating the ninety-day rule.

Form 8. Request for Execution

STATE OF NORTH CAROLINA

COUNTY OF _____

FILE NO. _____

IN THE GENERAL COURT OF JUSTICE

SUPERIOR COURT DIVISION

BEFORE THE CLERK

_____

Plaintiff

vs.

REQUEST FOR EXECUTION

_____

Defendant(s)

To the Clerk of the Superior Court of _____ County:

Whereas there is docketed in the Office of the Clerk of the Superior Court of _____ County a judgment in favor of the above-named plaintiff and against real property listed for taxes by the above-named defendant in the amount of $_____, with interest on this judgment at 8 percent per annum from _____, _____, all amounting to $_____ as of this date, which judgment constitutes a first lien prior to all other liens upon the property located in _____ Township, _____ County, North Carolina, and described as follows:

_____

[Insert full legal description].

And whereas the judgment remains unpaid and the amount now actually due thereon, including principal, interest, and costs, is $_____, and more than three months have elapsed since the judgment was filed in this court;

Therefore, pursuant to the authority vested in me by G.S. 105-375(i), I hereby request that execution upon the judgment be issued and that the liens upon the above-described property be foreclosed and the property be sold as provided by law.

This _____ day of _____, _____.

_____

Tax Collector of _____

[City] [County]

Form 9. Execution Order and Return on Execution

STATE OF NORTH CAROLINA

COUNTY OF _____

FILE NO. _____

IN THE GENERAL COURT OF JUSTICE

SUPERIOR COURT DIVISION

BEFORE THE CLERK

_____
Plaintiff

vs.   EXECUTION

_____
Defendant(s)

To the Sheriff of _____ County:

Whereas there is docketed in the Office of the Clerk of the Superior Court of _____ County a judgment in favor of the above-named plaintiff and against real property listed for taxes by the above-named defendant in the amount of $_____, with interest on this judgment at 8 percent per annum from _____, _____, all amounting to $_____ as of this date, which judgment constitutes a first lien prior to all other liens upon the property located in _____ Township, _____ County, North Carolina, and described as follows:

_____

[Insert full legal description].

And whereas the judgment remains unpaid and the amount now actually due thereon, including principal, interest, and costs, is $_____;

You are, therefore, commanded to satisfy the judgment by a sale of the property or so much thereof as is necessary to pay the judgment, principal, interest, and costs as they may appear at the time of the final report, and to return this execution within not more than ninety days from the date hereof to the undersigned.

This execution is issued this _____ day of _____, _____.

_____
Clerk of the Superior Court

RETURN ON EXECUTION

Received: _____, _____.

Served: _____, _____.

_____, Sheriff of
_____ County, North Carolina

By: _____, Deputy

Form 10. Pre-Execution Warning Letter to Owner

April 30, 2015
John Doe
123 Main Street
Raleigh, NC 12345

Dear Mr. Doe:

On _____ [date execution to be requested], _____ County will request the Clerk of Superior Court of _____ County to issue an Execution on the delinquent real property tax judgment filed on _____ [date judgment was docketed]. The Execution will direct the _____ County Sheriff to sell your real property at public auction. A copy of the Request for Execution that will be filed with the court is attached to this letter.

Once the Execution is issued, the sale of your real property can only be stopped by full payment of the amount indicated on the Request for Execution to the _____ County Sheriff in the form of cash, certified check, or money order. No personal checks will be accepted.

After _____ [date execution to be requested], the Sheriff of _____ County will advertise your property for sale for two weeks. If you do not pay before advertisement begins, advertising costs for each week will be added to the amount owed on your property.

Sincerely,

_____

_____ County Tax Collector

[Include copy of Request for Execution]

Although not required by G.S. 105-375, prior to obtaining executions from the court some local governments send property owners warnings of their intent to execute their judgments and sell the owners' properties. Form 10 is an example of a pre-execution warning letter, which should include a copy of the request for execution that the local government plans to file.

X. The *In Rem* Foreclosure Sale Process

In rem foreclosure sales are governed by the "execution sale" provisions found in G.S. Chapter 1, Article 29B, subject to a few exceptions unique to the *in rem* process.[90] The sale must be conducted by the sheriff, even if the foreclosure was prosecuted by a municipality rather than a county. The specific rules for execution sales may vary slightly from county to county because clerks of superior

---

90. G.S. 105-375(i) states that "the real property shall be sold by the sheriff in the same manner as other real property is sold under execution," with certain exceptions discussed above.

Form 11. Notice of Sale

STATE OF NORTH CAROLINA

COUNTY OF _____

FILE NO. _____

IN THE GENERAL COURT OF JUSTICE

SUPERIOR COURT DIVISION

BEFORE THE CLERK

_____
                Plaintiff

vs.   NOTICE OF SALE OF LAND UNDER EXECUTION

_____
              Defendant(s)

By virtue of an execution directed to the undersigned from the Superior Court of _____ County in the action entitled [insert name of plaintiff unit] vs. [defendants], I will, on _____, _____, at 12:00 noon, at the _____ County courthouse door, in the City [Town] of _____, sell the real property described below to the highest bidder for cash to satisfy the execution on that real property.

The execution was issued pursuant to judgment duly recorded in the office of the Clerk of the Superior Court for _____ County, in the amounts specified below.

The following described property is located in _____ Municipality, _____ County, North Carolina:

The real property is owned by [defendants] and described as follows:

_____

[Insert full legal description].

Amount due under judgment, including costs: $_____.

[Additional properties owned by the same taxpayers and also being foreclosed upon may be included in this notice].

The sale will be made subject to all outstanding taxes and all local improvement assessments against the above-described property not included in the judgment in the above-entitled cause.

The highest bidder at public sale shall be required to pay IN FULL the amount of the successful bid at the conclusion of the execution sale (subject to the confirmation of the sale as by law provided). The successful bid amount shall be paid in cash or certified funds (payable to the _____ County Sheriff's Department). The Sheriff's office may, in its discretion, determine and allow a reasonable time within which to deliver the successful bid amount to that office. The successful bidder shall also be responsible for the payment of any excise/transfer taxes due to the Register of Deeds office, and all recording fees at the appropriate time.

In accordance with G.S. 105-375(i), this Notice of Sale has been sent to the taxpayer and any lienholder(s) of record by first-class and certified mail, return receipt requested, and has been posted on the property. The Notice of Sale will be published as required by G.S. 1-339.52.

This the _____ day of _____, _____.

_____
Sheriff of _____ County

Form 12. Tax Collector Affidavit

STATE OF NORTH CAROLINA

COUNTY OF _____

IN THE GENERAL COURT OF JUSTICE

DISTRICT COURT DIVISION

FILE NO. _____ M _____

_____

Plaintiff

vs.

AFFIDAVIT OF POSTING PROPERTY

_____

Defendant(s)

I, _____ [Tax Collector], being duly sworn, do hereby attest as follows:

1. That I am the Tax Collector for _____ County, North Carolina.

2. That the property known as parcel #_____, having an address of _____, was posted with a Notice of Sale in the above-captioned matter by our staff on the _____ day of _____, 20__.

STATE OF NORTH CAROLINA

COUNTY OF _____

I, _____, a Notary Public of the County and State aforesaid, certify that _____ personally appeared before me this day and voluntarily acknowledged the due execution of the foregoing instrument.

Witness my hand and official stamp or seal, this the _____ day of _____, 20___.

_____

Notary Public

_____

My Commission Expires:

---

courts have authority to control procedural details that are not expressly created by statute.[91] With that in mind, below is an overview of the *in rem* foreclosure sale process.

A. Notice to Owners and Lienholders

Unlike other types of execution sales, personal service on the property owner is *not* required prior to an *in rem* execution sale. Instead, the sheriff is required to send notice via registered or certified mail, return receipt requested, to the taxpayer (meaning the current owner of record) at least thirty

---

91. G.S. 1-339.42.

days prior to the sale date.[92] The sheriff or the local government could choose to also provide personal service of this notice, but the statute makes it mandatory to mail that notice regardless.

Confusingly, the statute does not state that notice must be mailed to lienholders but later states that if the return receipt of the mailing to the taxpayer is not received, then the sheriff must make additional efforts to locate and notify the taxpayer *and* all lienholders through publication and posting signs on the property. This statutory reminder of the importance of giving notice to lienholders suggests that best practice is to mail notice of the execution sale to all lienholders at the same time notice is mailed to the taxpayer.

Form 11, on page 34, above, provides a sample notice of sale that can be used for both owners and lienholders.

Similarly, it makes good sense for the sheriff and/or the tax collector to post signs advertising the execution sale on the property itself in all cases. Although these signs are required only when the return receipt to the taxpayer is not received, they are often helpful in attracting bidders to the foreclosure sale and should be employed in every foreclosure.

As emphasized repeatedly in this publication, best practice is for the tax collector to document and confirm with the court all efforts to identify and notify parties with interests in the property. One method of accomplishing this goal is to file an affidavit with the court after posting notice of sale on the property. See Form 12, on page 35, above.

B. IRS Liens and Right of Redemption

Federal law requires that the foreclosing local government give special notice to the Internal Revenue Service (IRS) if that agency has a tax lien on the property being foreclosed upon.[93] Notice should be sent via certified or registered mail, return receipt requested, to:

> IRS, Attn: Manager, Centralized Lien Operation
> P.O. Box 145595, Stop 8420G NJS Team
> Cincinnati, OH 45250-5595[94]

The notice should include a copy of the judgment docketed against the property and copies of all IRS liens previously recorded against the property. See Form 13. Once the sale date is set, the tax collector should send a second notice to the IRS with that information.

If appropriate notice is provided to the IRS, then the federal tax lien on the property will be extinguished by the *in rem* foreclosure sale and the property will be sold free and clear of all liens.[95]

However, the federal government may still retain a "right of redemption" in the property that would authorize the IRS to buy the foreclosed property from the purchaser up to 120 days after the foreclosure sale.[96] It is unclear whether this right of redemption exists for North Carolina *in rem* tax

---

92. G.S. 105-375(i)(2).

93. 26 U.S.C. § 7425.

94. *See* I.R.S. Publication 786, Instructions for Preparing a Notice of Nonjudicial Sale of Property and Application for Consent to Sale (Apr. 2015), www.irs.gov/pub/irs-pdf/p786.pdf.

95. 26 U.S.C. § 6323 defers to state law with respect to the relative priority of federal tax liens versus local property tax liens on real property. North Carolina law makes local property tax liens senior to all other liens on real property except previously existing state tax liens. G.S. 105-356(a). The foreclosure of a senior lien extinguishes all junior liens if those junior liens have received notice of the foreclosure action. Dixieland Realty Co. v. Wysor, 272 N.C. 172 (1967). The IRS and other junior lienholders would have a claim on surplus sale proceeds that remain after the local government satisfies all taxes, costs, and fees owed on the property.

96. 26 U.S.C. § 7425(d). If the right of redemption exists, it would authorize the IRS to obtain ownership of the property from the buyer with or without consent from that party. The IRS would be required to

Form 13. IRS Notice

Dear IRS:

I have enclosed a copy of the judgment filed against _____. In approximately ninety days I will issue an Execution and set the Sale of Land Under Execution in the above-referenced case. I have also enclosed copies of your Federal Tax Lien as filed with the _____ County Clerk of Court on _____.

If you have any questions, please contact me at _____.

Sincerely,

_____

_____ County Tax Collector

---

foreclosure sales, but the question may be moot: experienced tax practitioners report that they have never seen the IRS exercise the right of redemption after a local government tax foreclosure sale.[97] So long as the local government gives the IRS appropriate notice, the existence of a federal tax lien and the IRS's possible right of redemption should not hinder an *in rem* foreclosure.

C. Posting and Advertising the Sale

Notice of the sale must be posted "in the area designated by the clerk of superior court for the posting of notices in the county in which the property is situated."[98] Usually this means someplace in the county courthouse. This posting must occur for at least twenty days prior to the sale date. As mentioned above, the sheriff or the tax office should also post sale notices on the property itself.

The sale must also be advertised in a local newspaper once a week for two consecutive weeks, with at least seven days in between the advertisements and with the last advertisement appearing within

---

compensate the buyer (who becomes an involuntary seller) at the price paid at the foreclosure sale plus 6 percent interest plus the net cost of maintaining the property (expenses incurred less any income received from the property during the buyer's period of ownership). 28 U.S.C. § 2410(d).

97. The IRS holds a right of redemption only in "non-judicial" sales of property. It is unclear whether North Carolina local government tax foreclosures are judicial or non-judicial. G.S. 1-339.1 excludes all tax foreclosures from the state definition of "judicial sales" for state law purposes. However, federal law determines whether a particular type of state foreclosure action is judicial or non-judicial for IRS purposes. United States v. Capobianco, 836 F.2d 808 (3d Cir. 1988). Because mortgage-style tax foreclosures under G.S. 105-374 require a traditional civil action and the opportunity for a hearing on the merits of the local government's claims, it seems likely that a federal court would conclude that foreclosures under G.S. 105-374 are judicial sales exempt from the IRS's right of redemption. In contrast, *in rem* foreclosures are expedited proceedings that do not include hearings on the merits, and thus they would likely be labeled non-judicial sales by a federal court. *See* Myers v. United States, 647 F.2d 591, 599 (5th Cir. 1981) (finding Louisiana's executory foreclosure sale not to be a judicial sale for IRS purposes because the process did not involve a "plenary judicial proceeding[] embodying the procedures associated with a complete and formal hearing on the merits"). If so, then the IRS would possess the right of redemption in all *in rem* foreclosure sales. While the existence of that right could scare away potential bidders or depress the price bidders are willing to pay for the property, the fact that the IRS appears never to have exercised this right following a tax foreclosure suggests that the concern is more theoretical than practical.

98. G.S. 1-339.52(a)(1).

ten days of the sale date.[99] The local government may combine multiple *in rem* foreclosure sales of different properties and different taxpayers in one advertisement.[100] Although not required, best practice is to include in the advertisements the amounts owed on the properties to be sold. Doing so is especially important if the local government intends to submit an initial bid at the amount owed on the property, because potential bidders will then know the minimum bid required to buy the property. See the next section for more details on offering initial bids.

Form 11 (see page 34, above), Notice of Sale, can be used for both the posting and the advertisement. The sheriff may collect the costs of notice and publication from the sale proceeds.[101] The local government should keep copies of this advertisement and all others published during the *in rem* process.

D. Auction and Sale

1. Submitting an Initial Bid

The actual foreclosure sale must be made to the "highest bidder for cash" on the courthouse steps.[102] Before the bidding begins, the local government must decide whether it will submit a bid of its own at the sale.

If the local government does not submit its own bid, the property might be sold for $1 or some other amount far below the taxes, interest, and costs owed on the property. The property will be sold free and clear of all tax liens included in the foreclosure, and the local government will most likely have to write off the unpaid amounts as uncollectible. Remember that even the taxpayer is permitted to buy the property at auction, and if the local government does not submit its own bid, that taxpayer might be able to buy the property free and clear of all tax liens for far less than the amount of those liens.

To avoid this result, many local governments will submit opening bids in their tax foreclosures at the amount of taxes, interest, costs, and fees owed on the properties. That way, if another party wants to buy the property, that party will be forced to bid enough to fully satisfy all amounts owed to the local government. But there is a risk to this strategy, of course. If nobody tops the government's initial bid, that government will be forced to buy the property.

Some local governments view the option of submitting an initial bid as an opportunity to set a "minimum" bid for other parties. They assume that they have the right to cancel the sale and try it again at a later date if nobody else bids on the property. That approach is incorrect. The "minimum" bid set by the local government is an actual bid, one that binds the local government to purchasing the property if it is not topped by a subsequent bid.

---

99. G.S. 105-339.52(a)(2), (b). This advertisement should be published in a newspaper that satisfies the requirements for legal advertising, if one exists. These requirements are described in G.S. 1-597. If no such newspaper exists in the county, then any paper with "general circulation" will suffice. "General circulation" means having some reasonable number of subscribers throughout the county. For more details on the choice of newspaper, see *Fundamentals*, chapter 9.

100. G.S. 105-375(I)(4). Each property and taxpayer must be separately identified in the combined advertisement.

101. G.S. 105-375(i)(3). This provision mentions only postage costs, not advertising costs. But seeing as all other advertising costs involved in the property tax foreclosure process may be charged to the taxpayer, it is reasonable to conclude that the pre-sale advertising costs can similarly be added to the amount owed on the property and collected at sale.

102. G.S. 1-339.51(5) (highest bidder for cash) and 1-339.44(a) (courthouse steps unless the property is located in two or more counties, in which case the sale may occur on the steps of the courthouse of any of those counties).

If the foreclosing government believes that it could make public use of the property as a park or administrative office or some other permissible activity, then the decision to submit an initial bid is an easy one. That is rarely the case, however, meaning that the local government must predict whether it would benefit financially from purchasing the property at foreclosure for the taxes and costs owed and holding it for sale at some point in the future. Perhaps the market for the property will improve in six months or a year, in which case there is more likely to be a buyer willing to pay at least what the local government is owed. The local government should also factor into this decision the loss of future property taxes during the time it owns the property.

If it seems unlikely that a future sale will produce substantially higher bids, then the local government might be better off allowing a third party to purchase the property at foreclosure for any amount—even an amount far below what is owed on the property—so that the property remains on the tax rolls in the hands of a new, and hopefully more responsible, owner.

For more details on the obligation of a local government that purchases property at a tax foreclosure sale, see section XIV, below.

2. Pre-Sale Disclosures

Although tax foreclosure sales are generally governed by the principle of *caveat emptor*—meaning "buyer beware"—local governments are wise to inform bidders about all information that might be relevant to their potential purchase of the property. These disclosures should include

1. taxes that will remain a lien on the property, most likely property taxes for the current or coming fiscal year that were not included in the foreclosure judgment;
2. environmental contamination or potential contamination, such as underground fuel storage tanks;
3. possible existence of unknown heirs in the case of property owned by the estate of a deceased taxpayer;
4. responsibility of the buyer to pay the county excise tax on conveyances[103] and any local land transfer taxes[104] necessary for the buyer to record the deed to the property that will be provided by the local government; and
5. the fact that the property is being sold "as is" with no warranties or representations as to the property or the status of title being delivered.

By disclosing these issues prior to the auction, a local government can minimize the chances of a high bidder being struck with buyer's remorse and reneging on a bid after being hit with an unwelcome surprise about the property.

As an example, here is the disclosure made by Durham County on its webpage advertising the properties to be sold in tax foreclosure:

> *Each property is being sold as-is, buyer beware, and it is the duty of any bidder to investigate the property on their own prior to making any bid. The information posted here*

---

103. G.S. 105-228.28, the authorizing statute for excise taxes, exempts transfers by local governments. However, a foreclosure sale is actually an involuntary transfer from the taxpayer to the high bidder. As a result, a purchase at a foreclosure sale is subject to county excise taxes. The general rate for excise taxes on conveyances $1 per $500 of purchase price. G.S. 105-228.30.

104. A handful of counties in eastern North Carolina have been granted authority to levy land transfer taxes in addition to the general excise tax on conveyances. *See* N.C. Sess. Laws ch. 1985, § 670 (Currituck County); ch. 1985, § 881 (Chowan County); ch. 1985, § 954 (Camden County); ch. 1989, § 786 (Pasquotank, Perquimans, and Washington counties).

about any tax foreclosure sale property (notice, minimum bid, redemption, structures and pictures) is for assistance only in this investigative process, and cannot and should not be relied upon solely by any bidder.[105]

The foreclosure attorneys for Mecklenburg County offers this warning to potential buyers as part of the "frequently asked questions" on their tax foreclosure webpage:

What is the status of title delivered by a tax foreclosure deed? Are there any warranties on the property?

The [County] will make it clear to all bidders present at the public sale that no representation or warranty of any kind is being made about the property or the status of title being delivered. Under state law, it is up to each bidder to carefully check out the title and status of the property being sold before placing either a public sale bid or an upset bid.[106]

3. The Auction Process

Assuming that a local government decides to submit its own bid for the property to make sure that the taxes and costs are covered, it can either submit that bid immediately once the sheriff announces the opening of the auction sale for a particular foreclosure or it can wait to see what other bidders do. If other bidders raise the sale price up to the amount of taxes and costs owed on the property, then the local government does not need to submit its own bid (unless the local government really wants to purchase the property for public use).

If a third party is the high bidder when the sheriff ends the auction, that bidder will be expected to pay the bid in cash. Because very few bidders will have that amount of cash with them at the auction, common practice is for the local government to permit the high bidder a couple of hours to obtain the cash or cash equivalent (cashier's check, certified check, etc.) and deliver it to the tax office. Best practice is to require some type of cash deposit from the high bidder at the sale to provide additional incentive to that party to produce the rest of the bid price within the required time frame.[107]

It is also good practice to get the contact information for all bidders at the auction so that the tax office can call the losing bidders to purchase the property if the high bidder fails to produce the purchase price as required. If a high bidder reneges on its bid and there are no other bidders interested in purchasing the property, the tax office will likely need to re-do the entire auction sale (and re-post and re-advertise the new sale date).[108]

If no third parties bid on the property, the local government may submit its own bid at whatever amount it desires. Usually that bid will be for the total amount owed on the property, but as discussed in section XIV, below, the amount of the local government's bid has no impact on its post-sale obligations. If the government chooses not to bid and the auction ends with no bidders, the sale can be rescheduled.[109]

---

105. http://dconc.gov/government/departments-f-z/tax-administration/foreclosure/property-tax-foreclosure-auction.

106. *See* www.rbcwblaw.com/tax-foreclosure-process.html.

107. Neither the *in rem* statute nor the execution sale statutes discuss the deposit requirement; those statutes assume that the high bidder will immediately pay the sale price in cash. But the mortgage-style foreclosure provision calls for a deposit of up to 20 percent. G.S. 105-374(m). That percentage deposit seems reasonable to apply to the *in rem* foreclosure process as well.

108. G.S. 1-339.69. The local government could sue the defaulting bidder for breach of contract, but that action is unlikely to be worth the time and effort involved.

109. The sale can be rescheduled within six days of the original sale date by re-posting the new date in the place where the clerk of court regularly posts notices of foreclosure sales. No advertising is required. If

Form 14. Report of Execution Sale

STATE OF NORTH CAROLINA

COUNTY OF _____

FILE NO. _____

IN THE GENERAL COURT OF JUSTICE

SUPERIOR COURT DIVISION

BEFORE THE CLERK

_____
Plaintiff

vs.

REPORT OF EXECUTION SALE

_____
Defendant(s)

Pursuant to the power and authority vested in me as Sheriff under an execution issued in this cause by the Honorable _____ _____, Clerk of the Superior Court of _____ County, after due advertisement of the sale in _____ [newspaper] on _____ [dates of advertisements] and mailing of notice of sale by certified mail to the owners at the last known address on _____ [date notice of sale was mailed] I offered for sale and sold at public auction for cash to the last and highest bidder the properties described in the execution at _____, at _____ o'clock _____.m., on the _____ day of _____, _____, to _____, the highest bidder, for $_____.

This _____ day of _____ _____,

_____

Sheriff of _____ County

HIGH BIDDER

Name: _____

Address: _____

Phone: _____

a. Report of Sale

The sheriff must file a report of sale with the clerk of court within five days after the initial auction sale.[110] This report must include the name of the winning bidder and the amount of the winning bid. See Form 14.

---

the new sale date is more than six days after the original sale date, the local government or the sheriff should re-post and re-advertise the new sale date as required by G.S. 1-339.52. Notice of the new date should also be mailed to all owners and lienholders as per G.S. 105-375(i)(2).

110. G.S. 1-339.63.

b. The Upset Bid Period

The General Statutes allow for "upset bids" in foreclosure sales after the initial auction sale order. The ten-day period in which a high bid can be topped and upset by another bidder begins the day after the report of sale is filed with the clerk of superior court.[111]

To qualify as an upset bid, a party must submit a new bid that tops the existing high bid by the greater of 5 percent of the high bid or $750. For example, if the existing high bid is $10,000, the lowest upset bid possible would be $10,750 (5 percent of $10,000 is $500, which is less than $750). If the existing high bid is $20,000, the lowest possible upset bid is $21,000 (5 percent of $20,000 is $1,000, which is greater than $750).

To offer an upset bid, the new bidder must submit to the clerk of court (not to the tax collector!) a notice of the bid plus a deposit that equals the greater of 5 percent or $750—in other words, the deposit should be at least the amount by which the upset bid exceeds the existing high bid.[112]

The clerk of court must then give notice of the upset bid to the tax collector using Form 15, the upset bid form required by the N.C. Administrative Office of the Courts. Technically the sheriff is the party conducting the sale, but practically the tax collector will be responsible for providing notice of the upset bid to the previous high bidder and the owners and lienholders of the property. If any of those parties wish to top the upset bid, they will need to file a new upset bid with the clerk of court that satisfies the 5 percent/$750 requirement mentioned above. Then the process will start all over again with a new Form 15 sent to the tax collector by the clerk and a new ten-day period for upset bids.

If the ten-day upset bid period ends without a new qualifying upset bid, the foreclosing government should contact the winning bidder and obtain the full amount of the bid (less the deposit paid to the clerk of court) in cash or certified/cashier's check. If the upset bid winner was the original high bidder at an auction sale, the tax collector simply needs to collect the difference between the winning upset bid the amounts previously paid by that bidder to the clerk of court (for the upset bids) and to the tax collector at the original auction sale. If the upset bid winner is a new bidder, the tax collector must return to the original auction high bidder the amounts paid by that party at the auction sale. Parties who submitted upset bids but did not win the property must obtain refunds of their upset bids from the clerk of court.

c. Confirmation of Sale, Deed, and Return of Execution

These documents are required to finalize the foreclosure sale after the upset bid period ends. Although the statutes suggest that the sheriff is responsible for creating all three, best practice is for the local government tax collector to prepare them to make sure they are accurate. All the sheriff will need to do is sign the documents.

i. Confirmation of Sale

G.S. 1-339.67 requires the clerk of superior court to confirm the sale before it may be "consummated"—in other words, before the property may be transferred to the high bidder. After talking with the clerk of court to make sure that the last upset bid period has ended with no additional bids, the tax collector can draft the order of confirmation for the clerk to sign and file. Once this order is filed, the tax collector can move on to the deed and the return of execution. See Form 16, on page 44, below.

---

111. G.S. 1-339.64. If the tenth day falls on a weekend or holiday, the upset bid period is extended to the next business day.

112. The notice must include the name and contact information for the bidder, the amount of the bid, and a reference to the new ten-day upset bid period that now begins due to the submission of the upset bid. G.S. 1-339.64(e).

Form 15. Upset Bid Report

STATE OF NORTH CAROLINA	File No.
_____ County	In The General Court Of Justice ☐ District ☐ Superior Court Division

Name Of Plaintiff(s)	
VERSUS	**NOTICE OF UPSET BID IN JUDICIAL SALE** **OR EXECUTION SALE** **NOTICE TO PERSON HOLDING THE SALE**
Name Of Defendant(s)	G.S. 1-339.25, -339.64

NOTICE OF UPSET BID

The undersigned, as the upset bidder, or as the attorney or agent for the upset bidder named below, gives notice of the filing of an upset bid in the above-referenced matter. The filing of this bid establishes a new sales price, and the sale shall remain open for a period of 10 days after this notice of Upset Bid is filed for the filing of additional upset bids as provided by law.

(**NOTE:** *The upset bid, as set forth below, must exceed the reported sale price or last upset bid by a minimum of 5%, but in any event must represent a minimum increase of at least $750.*)

Name And Address Of Upset Bidder	Name And Address Of Attorney Or Agent For Upset Bidder
Telephone No.	Telephone No.

Amount Of Last Previous Sale Or Upset Bid	Amount Of New Upset Bid	Deposit With Clerk (Greater Of $750 Or 5% Of Upset)
$	$	$ **See Note to Clerk below.**

Date Of Filing Of New Upset Bid	Signature

NOTICE TO PERSON HOLDING SALE

You are notified that, in the above-referenced matter, the Clerk of Superior Court of the above-referenced county is in receipt of a deposit by cash, certified check or cashier's check satisfactory to the Clerk, in an amount at least equal to the minimum required by G.S. 1-339.25 (judicial sales) or 1-339.64 (execution sales), together with the above timely-filed Notice of Upset Bid. **YOU ARE DIRECTED TO MAIL WRITTEN NOTICE** of the upset bid by first class mail to the last known address of the last prior bidder, the current record owner(s) of the property, and to all other persons or entities you may deem appropriate.

Date	Signature	☐ Deputy CSC ☐ Assistant CSC ☐ Clerk Of Superior Court

Last Day For Next Upset Bid	Minimum Amount Of Next Upset Bid	Amount Of Deposit For Next Minimum Upset Bid
	$	$

NOTE TO CLERK: *Deliver upset bid deposit along with completed form AOC-G-120 to the bookkeeper.*

Form 16. Order of Confirmation

STATE OF NORTH CAROLINA

COUNTY OF _____

FILE NO. _____

IN THE GENERAL COURT OF JUSTICE

SUPERIOR COURT DIVISION

BEFORE THE CLERK

_____

Plaintiff

vs.

ORDER OF CONFIRMATION

_____

Defendant(s)

This matter was heard before the undersigned Clerk of the Superior Court upon the report of _____ _____, Sheriff of _____ County, filed on the _____ day of _____, _____, and it appearing from the report that the Sheriff did, on the _____ day of _____, _____, offer for sale the real property described in the Execution issued in this action, after due advertisement in accordance with law,

[either]

at which sale _____ became the last and highest bidder for the amount of $_____; and it further appearing that the sale was regularly and lawfully conducted and that more than ten days have elapsed since the report of the sale was filed and no increased bids or exceptions have been filed with respect thereto;

[or if an upset bid was submitted]

that the sale was regularly and lawfully conducted and that _____ offered the last upset bid in the amount of $_____, and that more than ten days have elapsed since the last upset bid, motion for resale, or resale at which sale _____ became the last and highest bidder for the amount of $_____; and it further appearing that the sale was regularly and lawfully conducted and that more than ten days have elapsed since the report of the sale was filed and no increased bids or exceptions have been filed with respect thereto.*

It is, therefore, ordered that the sale be confirmed, and the Sheriff is hereby ordered to deliver to the purchaser** a deed to the real property in fee simple, upon receipt of the purchase price; and after deducting the expenses of the sale and fees allowed him or her by law, the Sheriff is ordered to pay the proceeds of the sale to this court.

This the _____ day of _____, _____.

_____

Clerk of the Superior Court

*If the governing unit's bid has been assigned, add "and _____, having been assigned the bid of the [City] [County] of _____, by action of the [City Council] [Board of County Commissioners] taken on, _____, _____."

**If there has been an assignment, substitute "assignee" for "purchaser." See Form 19 for assignment of bid.

ii. Deed

A deed is needed to transfer the property to the high bidder (which might be the local government; see section XIV, below). As Form 17, on pages 46–47, below, indicates, the deed is between the sheriff and the high bidder, even though the actual (involuntary) seller/grantee is the taxpayer. The deed should indicate that the property is subject to a lien for property taxes for the current or coming fiscal year if those taxes were not included in the foreclosure judgment because they were not a lien on the property when that judgment was docketed. (See section XV, below, for more on which tax liens survive a foreclosure.) The sheriff, along with the chair of the county commissioners (if a county conducts the foreclosure) or the mayor or the chair of the city council (if a city conducts the foreclosure), should sign the deed. If the county and city conduct the foreclosure jointly, then officials from both local governments should sign the deed. All signatures on the deed signatures should be notarized.

The deed should not be delivered to the buyer until after the tax collector has confirmed that the buyer has paid the full sale price either to the sheriff, the local government, or the clerk of court.[113] If the high bidder fails to make good on the winning bid, the local government should of course keep the deposit submitted by that bidder. Another auction sale must be scheduled and notice again provided to all interested parties as described above. As mentioned previously, the local government is authorized to sue the defaulting bidder for any losses incurred due to the need to re-sell the property, but such a lawsuit is not likely to be worth the cost and effort.[114]

iii. Return of Execution

The final document to be signed by the sheriff is the "return of execution" form that documents the fact that the sheriff's office has fulfilled its obligations under the execution. This form can simply be a signature from the sheriff on the original execution. See Form 9, on page 32, in section IX, above. The return of execution should be filed with the court along with the sale proceeds collected from the sheriff and/or the winning bidder plus a distribution report that instructs the clerk how those proceeds should be distributed.

XI. Distribution of Proceeds

After collecting the full bid amount from the winning bidder, the local government must document how it wishes the clerk of superior court to distribute the funds to it, to other local governments involved in the foreclosure, and to the sheriff for sale costs. See Form 18, on page 48, below, for a sample distribution report used by Orange County. (Note that this form assumes that the sheriff retained the service fees and commission due his office at the close of the initial sale. That is common practice but not required.)

---

113. G.S. 1-339.69(b) allows the high bidder ten days to pay the purchase price after "tender of the deed"—in other words, after the deed is delivered to the high bidder. However, best practice is to demand full payment from the high bidder *before* delivering the deed.

114. G.S. 1-339.69.

Form 17. Sheriff's Deed

STATE OF NORTH CAROLINA

COUNTY OF _____

SHERIFF'S DEED (PAGE 1 OF 2)

This deed, made this _____ day of _____, _____, by and between _____, Sheriff of _____ County, North Carolina, (the "Sheriff"), and _____ [High Bidder/Buyer] (the "Buyer"),

WITNESSETH

That whereas the Sheriff, being duly authorized by an Execution issued upon a judgment docketed in the office of the Clerk of the Superior Court for _____ County in a proceeding entitled "_____ v. _____," (File No. _____), and after due advertisement in accordance with law, did offer for sale and did sell, at public auction for cash to the highest bidder, at the courthouse door in _____ County, on the _____ day of _____, real property herein described, when and where _____ became the last and highest bidder for the same at the price of $_____; and

**Whereas the sale has been confirmed by order of the Superior Court, and the Buyer has fully paid the amount of the bid to the Sheriff;

Now, therefore, in consideration of the premises and in further consideration of the sum of _____ dollars ($_____) in hand paid to the Sheriff by the Buyer, receipt of which is hereby fully acknowledged, the Sheriff does hereby give, grant, bargain, sell, and convey unto the Buyer, his or her heirs and assigns, all of the lot, tract, or parcel of real estate in _____ Township, _____ County, North Carolina, and being more particularly bounded and described as follows:

_____

[Insert full legal description.]

For more particular description, see deed from _____ to _____, recorded in Deed Book _____, page _____, in the Office of the Register of Deeds of _____ County.

This conveyance is subject to city and county property taxes for _____, the payment of which shall be assumed by the Buyer. To have and to hold the above-described premises and all privileges and appurtenances thereunto appertaining, to the Buyer, his or her heirs and assigns, to only their use and forever free and clear of all encumbrances except all outstanding city and county taxes and all local improvement assessments against the above-described property not included in the judgment in the above-entitled cause in as full and ample manner as the Sheriff is authorized and empowered to convey the same;

In witness whereof, the Sheriff has hereunto set his hand and seal, the day and year first above written.

_____ (Seal)

Sheriff

_____ (Seal)

(continues on next page)

Form 17. Sheriff's Deed (continued)

SHERIFF'S DEED (PAGE 2 OF 2)

I, _____, notary public in and for the County of _____, do hereby certify that _____, Sheriff of _____ County, personally appeared before me this day and acknowledged the due Execution of the foregoing deed as his or her own act and deed.

Witness my hand and official seal, this _____ day of _____, _____.

_____
                Notary Public

My commission expires _____, _____

**If the city and/or county was the high bidder and has assigned its bid, the following language should be added to the deed where indicated:

Whereas _____ did, on _____, _____, by proper resolution of the [Board of County Commissioners] [City Council] assign its bid to _____, party of the second part, for the sum of $_____; and

[Also include the following language if the county and city jointly bid and assigned their bid:]

The City of _____, _____ County, joins in the Execution of this deed for the purpose of assigning and does hereby assign, transfer, and deliver to said party of the second part, his or her heirs and assigns, its bid to the above-described property which it made at the aforesaid public sale on the _____ day of _____, _____, together with all right, title, interest, and estate in the property to which it is entitled by reason of its bid.]

[Mayor of the City of_____]

[Chair of the Board of Commissioners of _____ County]

Form 18. Distribution Report to Clerk of Court

Owner Name: _____   File Number: ____ M ____

Date Judgment Docketed: _____   PIN #: _____

IN REM FORECLOSURE DISBURSEMENT SUMMARY

HIGH BID AMOUNT		$ _____
Judgment Total	$ _____	to Tax Collector
Certified Mail for Notice of Sale	$ _____	to Tax Collector
Advertising Fee for Notice of Sale	$ _____	to Tax Collector
8% Post-Judgment Interest to Date of Sale	$ _____	to Tax Collector
SUBTOTAL TO TAX COLLECTOR:		$ _____
Sheriff Commission and Service Fee	$ _____	to Sheriff
SUBTOTAL TO SHERIFF (PREVIOUSLY PAID):		$ _____
Execution and Filing Fee	$ _____	to Clerk of Court
Excess Bid Proceeds	$ _____	to Clerk of Court (Surplus Funds)
Funds on Deposit with Clerk from Upset Bid Filings	$ _____	to Clerk of Court (Surplus Funds)
SUBTOTAL TO CLERK OF COURT:		$ _____
TOTAL DISBURSED:		$ _____

TO THE CLERK OF COURT:

YOU WILL RECEIVE A CHECK FROM THE FINANCE OFFICE IN THE AMOUNT OF $_____, WHICH IS THE BALANCE DUE ON THE BID LESS THE SHERIFF'S COMMISSION AND SERVICE FEES THAT WERE PAID AT THE TIME OF SALE.

PLEASE CUT A CHECK TO THE _____ COUNTY TAX COLLECTOR IN THE AMOUNT OF $_____ RE: ____ M ____.

YOU WILL RETAIN $_____ IN EXECUTION AND FILING FEES AND $_____ IN SURPLUS FUNDS.

Distributions should be made in this order:

1. To the sheriff for any costs incurred during the sale (advertising, service of notice, etc.) and for the sale fee (5 percent of the first $500 of the winning bid, 2.5 percent of any remaining bid amount above $500).[115]
2. To the local governments that participated in the foreclosure for post-judgment interest at 8 percent per annum on the total amount of the judgment. (See section VII.C.5, above, for details on how to calculate post-judgment interest.)

_____

115. G.S. 7A-311(a)(3). Note that often the sheriff will retain this fee from the sale proceeds immediately upon concluding the foreclosure auction.

3. To the local governments that participated in the foreclosure for all taxes, interest, costs, and fees plus any nuisance abatement costs included in the foreclosure.[116]

4. To the local governments that participated in the foreclosure that have liens for special assessments or minimum housing code enforcement costs (commonly called "demolition liens").[117]

If surplus sale proceeds remain after these distributions, they should be given to the clerk of court for a distribution to the taxpayer or to creditors who held junior liens on the property.[118] The local government is not permitted to keep any sale proceeds in excess of the taxes, interests, costs, and other amounts owed on the property. In other words, a local government is not permitted to make a profit on a tax foreclosure.[119]

If the foreclosure sale does not produce enough funds to cover all of the local government debts, some of those debts must be paid on a pro-rata basis (in other words, in proportion to their share of the total amounts included in the judgment) and debts of junior priority will not be paid. Here is an example of how that might work in practice:

> Assume Carolina County and Blue Devil City jointly pursue *in rem* foreclosure on 123 Main Street. The judgment docketed includes the following debts:
>
> 1. $3,000 in taxes, interest, and costs for 2012 taxes owed to Carolina County;
> 2. $2,000 in taxes, interest, and costs for 2013 taxes owed to Blue Devil City; and
> 3. $1,000 in special assessments and interest for construction of a sewer line by Blue Devil City in 2010.
>
> The local governments decide not to submit an initial bid and the property is sold at auction for $3,000. No upset bids are received and the sale is finalized 100 days after the judgment was docketed. Here's how the sale proceeds should be distributed:
>
> 1. Sheriff's fees: 5 percent of the first $500 and then 2.5 percent of the remaining $2,500, for a total of $87.50.
> 2. Post-judgment interest on $6,000 for 100 days at 8 percent per year, for a total of $131.50. The two local governments should share this pro-rata. In this case, the split is 50/50 because each local government is owed 50 percent of the total judgment ($3,000 in property taxes to the county, $3,000 in property taxes plus special assessments to the city).

---

116. G.S. 105-356(a)(2) makes all local property tax liens on real property of "equal dignity," meaning that they have the same priority and are paid at the same time regardless of when the tax liens arose. For example, assume a county and a city jointly foreclose on Parcel A. The county has a 2008 tax lien on the parcel and the city has a 2010 tax lien on the parcel. Both tax liens should be paid at the same time following the tax foreclosure sale. G.S. 153A-140 and 160A-193 make county and city nuisance abatement costs the equivalent of property taxes for collection purposes.

117. G.S. 153A-200(c) and 160A-233(c) make county and city special assessments collectible as property taxes but at a junior priority. G.S. 160A-433(6)(a) does the same for county and city housing code enforcement costs.

118. If other creditors and the taxpayer disagree over how those excess funds should be distributed, the clerk will be required to hold a "special proceeding" under G.S. 1-339.71 to resolve the dispute. Happily, the local government is not required to participate in that procedure.

119. Note that a local government is permitted to keep surplus proceeds if it buys the property at a tax foreclosure sale and later sells it as surplus property. See section XIV.F.3, below.

Subtracting these two amounts from the $3,000 sale proceeds leaves $2,781.

1. The property taxes, interests, and costs owed to each local government have equal priority. Because the total of these debts ($5,000) is more than the remaining sale proceeds, the local governments will be paid pro-rata. The county is owed 3/5 of that amount (60 percent) and the city is owed 2/5 of that amount (40 percent). As a result, the county should receive 60 percent of the remaining sale funds, which equals $1,668.60. The city gets the remaining 40 percent, which equals $1,122.40. The property is sold free and clear of all liens for the taxes included in the foreclosure despite the fact that the taxes were not paid in full at the foreclosure sale. The local governments no longer have any Machinery Act collection remedies for these taxes.
2. There are no funds remaining to pay the city's special assessment debt. The property is sold free and clear of the special assessment lien and the city no longer has any Machinery Act collection remedies for that debt.

XII. Distribution of Proceeds When a Senior Lien Exists

As discussed in section II, question 4, above, local property tax liens are senior to and paid before almost all other liens that might exist on real property. The only type of lien that might be senior to a local property tax lien is a tax lien held by the State of North Carolina (usually for state income taxes). A state tax lien is senior to a local property tax lien if the state tax lien was recorded with the register of deeds or filed with the local clerk of court prior to the property tax lien arising on January 1 of the year for the tax is levied.

If the property is subject to a state tax lien that was recorded or filed prior to January 1 of the earliest property tax year included in the foreclosure, then that state tax lien must be paid before any property taxes are paid. If the sale does not produce enough funds to pay off both the state and local taxes, the property still will be sold free and clear of the local property tax liens.

For example, assume that Parcel A is subject to a $10,000 tax lien for 2008 North Carolina income taxes that was filed on February 1, 2010. Carolina County holds property tax liens on Parcel A for years 2011 through 2015 that total $5,000. The state tax lien is senior to the local property tax liens. The county forecloses on the property and the sale produces only $8,000. After paying off the sheriff, the sale funds must first be paid to the senior state tax lien. No funds would remain to pay the local taxes, but Parcel A is sold free and clear of those liens regardless.[120]

Distribution is more complicated when the local government holds property tax liens that both pre-date and post-date the state tax lien. In this situation, some of the local government's property taxes will be senior to the state tax lien and some will be junior.

Assume that Carolina County forecloses on Parcel B for 2011 and 2012 taxes. Parcel B is also subject to a state income tax lien of $10,000 that was recorded in March of 2011. The county's 2011

---

120. It is unclear whether the property would be sold subject to the unpaid portion of the senior state tax lien. Generally, the foreclosure of a junior lien does not extinguish a senior lien. G.S. 1-339.68. However, the Machinery Act states that property sold at a tax foreclosure sale must be sold "free and clear" of all liens, with no exception for senior liens. Based on the statutory interpretation principle of "the specific trumps the general," the author believes that the specific provision in the tax foreclosure statute would trump the general rules for execution sales. If so, then senior state tax liens are in fact extinguished by the foreclosure of junior local property tax liens, even if the sale does not produce enough funds to satisfy the state taxes entirely.

property tax lien is senior to the state tax lien because it arose on January 1, 2011, before the state tax lien was recorded. But the county's 2012 tax lien, which arose on January 1, 2012, is junior to the state tax lien.

After payment of the sheriff's costs, the sale proceeds first should be applied to the county's 2011 property tax lien, then to the state tax lien, and finally to the county's 2012 property tax lien. The property will be sold free and clear of the property tax liens regardless of whether there are enough funds to satisfy them entirely.[121]

XIII. Payment Prior to Sale

An *in rem* foreclosure must be terminated if all taxes, interest, costs, and fees are paid prior to the termination of a pending upset bid period.[122] These payments are usually made by the taxpayer, but payment of the appropriate amount by any party must stop the foreclosure. Contrary to a persistent myth, payment by a third party of all of the taxes, interest, and fees owed in the foreclosure does not entitle that third party to ownership of the property.[123]

If a foreclosure is stopped due to payment prior to the culmination of the foreclosure sale, ownership of the property remains in the name of the taxpayer. Once an execution is issued, the costs must include both the execution fee and the sheriff's fee. The execution fee is $25.[124] The sheriff's statutory sales fees, discussed in section XI, above, are 5 percent of the first $500 plus 2.5 percent of all amounts over $500.[125] The sheriff's fees are calculated on the total of all taxes, interest, and other costs and must be paid to stop the foreclosure process even if the sale does not occur.

Note that the amount required to terminate a foreclosure does not increase along with increased bids submitted during the sale and upset bid process. Regardless of how high the bids may have risen, only taxes, pre- and post-judgment interest, and fees must be paid to terminate the foreclosure and maintain the taxpayer's ownership of the property.

---

121. The Machinery Act may provide the opportunity for local governments to take a more aggressive approach to state tax liens. G.S. 105-356(a)(2) mandates that the property tax liens of all local governments have "equal dignity," meaning equal priority. This means that property tax liens from different years all have the same priority. If one property tax lien has priority over a state tax lien (because it arose prior to the state tax lien), then all subsequent property tax liens could share that same priority and could be paid before the state tax lien (even if one or more of those property tax liens arose after the state tax lien). State courts have not yet addressed this argument.

122. G.S. 1-339.57.

123. Parties that already hold an interest in a property may obtain additional interests by payment of the taxes owed on that property. G.S. 105-363(b) gives a co-tenant who pays more than his/her ownership share of the taxes owed on jointly owned property a lien against his/her co-tenants in the amount of those "excess" taxes. G.S. 105-384 gives a remainderman a cause of action against the life tenant if the remainderman pays the taxes owed on the property while the life tenancy survives. And G.S. 105-386 gives a lienholder who pays the taxes on the property an additional lien with super-priority on the property in the amount of taxes paid. But the Machinery Act does not authorize a third party with no existing interest in a property any new interest simply due to the payment of taxes owed on that property.

124. G.S. 7A-308(a)(5).

125. G.S. 7A-311(a)(3).

The right to terminate a foreclosure ends when the upset bid period (or the last of many upset bid periods) ends. Unlike some other states, North Carolina does not offer taxpayers any "right of redemption" after a foreclosure sale is completed.[126]

The amount a taxpayer or a third party would need to pay depends entirely on when in the process the taxpayer or the third party attempts to terminate the foreclosure. Consider this example:

Suzy Seahawk's property is being foreclosed upon by Carolina County. When the judgment is docketed on May 1, Suzy owes $10,000 in taxes, Machinery Act interest, and costs (everything except the sheriff's fee). How much Suzy needs to pay to terminate the foreclosure depends on when she pays.

1. Suzy pays on May 1, the date the judgment is docketed: Suzy needs to pay only the $10,000, because no additional interest or costs have accrued on the property.

2. Suzy pays on May 31: Suzy needs to pay the $10,000 plus 8 percent post-judgment interest for the thirty days that have passed since the judgment was docketed. That amounts to an additional $65.70, for a total payment amount of $10,065.70.[127]

3. Suzy pays on August 29. The execution was issued and delivered to the sheriff for sale on August 15. Suzy needs to pay the $10,000 plus 8 percent post-judgment interest for the 120 days that have passed since the judgment was docketed plus the execution fee plus the sheriff's sales fees on the taxes, interest, and costs. Daily post-judgment interest amounts to $262.80. The execution fee is $25. The sheriff's fees are calculated on the total taxes, interest, and costs (other than the sheriff's fee) of $10,287.80: 5 percent for the first $500 plus 2.5 percent for the remaining $9,787.80. The total sheriff's fee is $269.70.[128] The grand total owed by Suzy is $10,557.50.

4. Suzy pays on November 1, at which time the foreclosure sale has been held and numerous upset bids have been submitted. The pending upset bid to buy the property is $450,000. Suzy would still be required to pay only the $10,000 in taxes, pre-judgment interest, and costs plus post-judgment interest plus the execution fee and the sheriff's fee on that total. 185 days of post-judgment interest amounts to $405.15. The execution fee is $25. That means that the sheriff's sale fee is calculated on $10,430.15, resulting in a fee of $273.26. The total amount Suzy must pay to terminate the foreclosure is $10,703.41. Note that the current high bid ($450,000) in the foreclosure sale has no effect on the amount Suzy must pay. The tax office is not losing money, despite the loss of a much higher bid; any funds in excess of the amount owed by Suzy would be turned over to the clerk of superior court and then distributed to either other creditors or to Suzy.

5. Suzy tries to pay on November 10, two days after the final upset bid period ends. Suzy is too late; she has lost her right to terminate the foreclosure. The sheriff and the tax office must collect the sale price from the high bidder and transfer the property to that bidder via a sheriff's deed. Suzy no longer has any rights in the property.

---

126. For example, Texas permits a taxpayer to redeem foreclosed property within two years of the sale by paying all taxes, interest, and costs plus a premium of 25 to 50 percent. 1 Tex. Tax Code § 34.21.

127. Post-judgment interest should be calculated on a daily basis. Annual interest of 8 percent equates to daily interest of .0219 percent. The calculation in this example should be $10,000 x .000219 x 30 = $65.70.

128. 5 percent of $500 is $25. Add to that 2.5 percent of the remaining amount owed(0.25 x ($10,287.80 - $500) = $244.70, for a total sheriff's fee of $269.70.

XIV. Local Government as Purchaser

A local government is free to purchase property at a tax foreclosure auction. This might occur by default when a local government enters an initial bid at the amount of taxes and costs owed on the property (see section X.D.1, above) and no other parties offer bids. Or it might happen when the local government affirmatively wishes to purchase the property being sold and successfully outbids another party. Either way, the local government will become the owner of the property (assuming the government does not assign its bid[129]) and its ownership of the property will be governed by G.S. 105-376.[130]

Below are a few important points to keep in mind if a local government is the high bidder.

A. Purchase Price

The local government is required to pay only that amount that would not be distributed to it and other local governments for taxes, interest, and costs. Normally that will require payment only of the sheriff's fees owed on the government's bid (5 percent of the first $500, 2.5 percent of the rest).[131] If the local government bids more than what was owed on the property (because it wanted to outbid other parties and take ownership of the property), that local government would be required to pay to the court the amount of the bid that exceeded the taxes, interest, and costs owed on the property.

Assume Carolina County forecloses on Parcel A and offers an initial ("minimum") bid of $5,000, the amount of taxes, interest, and costs owed on the property. $2,000 of that amount is owed to Blue Devil City for its taxes, interests, and costs. If no other party bids on the property, then Carolina

---

129. G.S. 105-376, the statute that governs purchase of property at a tax foreclosure by a local government, authorizes a local government that was the winning high bidder to assign its bid "by private sale" for any amount equal to or greater than the local government's winning bid. In other words, the government may transfer its winning bid to another party without triggering the need for an upset bid period. That other party would then be the high bidder and, assuming it made prompt payment of the bid, would become owner of the property.

130. Note that this statute applies only when property is purchased by a local government unit, not by an employee or elected official of the local government. Technically, an employee or elected official of the foreclosing local government could buy property at a tax foreclosure sale without violating state law. Although G.S. 14-234 prohibits local government officials from acquiring property through a contract with that local government, a tax foreclosure sale is a forced, involuntary sale by the taxpayer and not a contract with the foreclosing local government. As a result, G.S. 14-234 would likely not apply and the purchase would be permissible.

That said, there are excellent reasons for a local government to discourage (or in the case of employees, prohibit) its elected officials from bidding at its own foreclosure sales. Most importantly, the optics are terrible. Public reaction would almost certainly be loud and negative were an employee or elected official of the foreclosing government to purchase the foreclosed property. More substantive legal concerns could arise if the purchaser relied on "insider" information. G.S. 14-234.1 prohibits an official from obtaining property about which the officials possesses "information which was made known to him in his official capacity and which has not been made public." There should be no insider information available, because best practice is for the foreclosing government to share all information it has about the foreclosed property with all potential bidders. See section X.D.2, above. But if such information existed and was used by a local government employee or elected official to purchase the property, the transaction would be illegal.

131. The only amounts that a local government might be required to pay at the sale would be the court's filing fee and the execution fee if those fees were not previously paid. The filing fees are minimal: $6 for the first page and 25 cents for each additional page. G.S. 7A-308 (a)(11). The execution fee is $25. G.S. 7A-308(a)(5). The clerk of court may permit the local government to wait to pay the filing fee until either the taxes are paid or the property is sold, whichever comes first, as permitted by G.S. 105-375(b). The clerk may also defer the execution fee. If this happens, then the local government would need to pay both fees when it purchases the property.

County is the winning bidder and is not required to pay anything other than the sheriff's fees (and the court fees if not previously paid).

Assume Carolina County forecloses on Parcel B and decides that it wants to purchase the property for use as an addition to a neighboring county park. The county submits an initial bid of $5,000, the amount of taxes, interest, and costs owed on the property, $2,000 of which is owed to Blue Devil City. Tommy Tar Heel then offers a bid of $7,000. The county ups its bid to $7,500 and wins the auction. To finalize the sale, the county must pay $2,500 (the difference between its winning bid and the taxes, costs, and interest owed on the property) to the clerk of superior court plus the sheriff's fees on the $7,500 bid (and the court fees if not previously paid). The clerk must then determine how to distribute those excess funds to either the taxpayer or to creditors holding junior liens on the property.

B. Assignment of Bid

G.S. 105-376(a) authorizes a local government to "assign" (in other words, sell) its winning bid to another party at a private sale (meaning no public auction is required) for any amount equal to or greater than the amount of the winning bid. This process can be quicker and less onerous than a subsequent public sale of the foreclosed property by the local government. (See section XIV.D, below, for more on that process.) Note that the assignment of a bid requires action by the local government's governing board; it cannot be accomplished by the tax collector alone. Form 19 can be used to document an assignment of bid.

C. "Hold for the Benefit of Taxing Units"

If the local government takes ownership of the property at the close of the foreclosure process, that government holds the property for the benefit of all local governments that were owed taxes or other debts collectible as taxes relating to the property.[132]

This requirement obligates the purchasing government to reimburse the other local governments for their interests in the property if the property is later sold. (See section XIV.D, below, for more on subsequent sales and reimbursement of other local governments.)

If the local government chooses instead to hold the property for public use, G.S. 105-376(b) requires that local government to "make settlement" with the other governments "in such amount as may be agreed upon by the governing bodies." If the local governments cannot agree on how much the purchasing government should pay the others for their taxes and other debts owed on the property, the dispute must be resolved by the state superior court.

D. Subsequent Sale: Private or Public?

Most often the purchasing government wants to sell the foreclosed property as soon as possible. In general, the same rules that govern the disposition of any local property govern the sale of property purchased by a local government at a tax foreclosure sale.[133] Surplus government property may be sold to the general public by (1) sealed bid, (2) upset bid, or (3) public auction.[134]

---

132. Special assessments, nuisance abatement costs, housing code enforcement costs, ambulance services fees, and solid waste fees billed with property taxes may all be collected as property taxes in a foreclosure action. See section VII.C.2, above.

133. G.S. 105-376(c).

134. A detailed discussion about the laws governing the disposition of public property is beyond the scope of this publication. For more on this topic, see Normal Houston, *North Carolina Local Government*

Form 19. Assignment of Bid

STATE OF NORTH CAROLINA

COUNTY OF _____

FILE NO. _____

IN THE GENERAL COURT OF JUSTICE
SUPERIOR COURT DIVISION
BEFORE THE CLERK

_____
Plaintiff

vs.

ASSIGNMENT

_____
Defendant(s)

The [County] [City] of _____ was the last and highest bidder for that certain tract or parcel of real property described in the Execution in the above-entitled cause at a sale held on the _____ day of _____, _____, and I, _____ _____, as [Mayor of the City] [Chair of the Board of Commissioners of the County], pursuant to authority vested in me by resolution of the [City Council] [Board of County Commissioners] dated _____, _____, do hereby, in consideration of _____'s promise to pay the sum of $_____, the amount of the bid, to the Sheriff upon confirmation of the sale, sell, set over, transfer, and assign the [County's] [City's] bid made at the sale unto _____, his or her heirs and assigns; and _____ _____, Sheriff in the sale, is hereby instructed to execute and deliver a deed conveying the real property to _____, his or her heirs and assigns, upon the confirmation of the sale and upon payment to him or her by _____ of the purchase price.

Witness my hand and seal, this _____ day of _____, _____.

_____ (Seal)
[Mayor of the City of_____]

[Chair of the Board of Commissioners of _____ County]

Attested by: _____
Clerk to the Board (Seal)

NORTH CAROLINA

_____ County

I, _____, Notary Public for said County and State, certify that _____ personally appeared before me this day, and being by me duly sworn, acknowledged that he or she is clerk to the board of _____ [County] [a municipal corporation] and that by authority duly given and as the act of the [County] [Municipality], the foregoing instrument was signed in its name by the [Mayor] [Chair of the Board of Commissioners], sealed with its official seal, and attested by himself or herself as Clerk to the Board.

Witness my hand and seal, this _____ day of _____, _____.

(Seal)

_____
Notary Public

My commission expires _____, _____.

If the purchasing government sells the property through any of these types of public sales, there are no restrictions on the selling price. Any party (including the former owner) may purchase the property for any price so long as the selling government follows the general requirements for the disposal of public property.

Property purchased by a local government at a tax foreclosure sale may also be sold by private sale to the former owner or to any other party who previously had an interest in the property (a mortgage lender, for example).[135] In a private sale, the general public is not given the opportunity to bid on the property. This type of sale is permitted only if the sale price is equal to or greater than the total amount of taxes, interest, and costs (not including special assessments) owed to all local governments on the property. This amount must include taxes that have become a lien on the property (or would have become a lien on the property but for the purchase by the local government) since the foreclosure sale.[136]

Consider again the example above in which Carolina County purchases at its own foreclosure sale Parcel A, on which $5,000 of taxes, interest, and costs were owed. $2,000 of those taxes, interest, and costs were owed to Blue Devil City. The foreclosure began in late 2015 and the county finalizes the foreclosure sale in early 2016.

Tommy Tar Heel, the taxpayer who owned Parcel A before the foreclosure sale, contacts the county and asks what he can do to get his property back. Although it is too late to terminate the foreclosure, the county could sell the property back to Tommy at a private sale. The general public would not receive notice of the sale or the opportunity to bid on the property. The minimum price for a private sale of the property back to Tommy would be $5,000, the total amount of taxes, interest, and costs owed to the county and the city *plus* the estimated 2016 taxes for both the city and the county that are now a lien on the property.[137] This is true regardless of whether the city participated in the foreclosure and regardless of what price Carolina County actually bid for the property at the foreclosure sale. The county could negotiate a higher price with Tommy, of course; the Machinery Act merely sets a floor for the private sale.

Contracting: Quick Reference and Related Statutes (UNC School of Government, 2014), available for purchase here: http://shopping.netsuite.com/s.nl/c.433425/it.A/id.5335/.f?sc=7&category=29.

135. G.S. 105-376(c).

136. Property taxes become liens on real property automatically every January 1. G.S. 105-355(a). Property owned by the federal or state government or by or a local government as of January 1 is exempt from property taxes. G.S. 105-278.1. As a result, if a local government purchases a property at a tax foreclosure sale and holds it as of January 1, that property would normally be exempt from property taxes unless it is transferred to a taxable owner prior to July 1 of that calendar year. G.S. 105-285(d). However, G.S. 105-376 instructs tax collectors to ignore the potential exempt status of property purchased by a local government when determining the minimum sale price for a private sale to the former owner or to a party that previously had an interest in the property.

137. If the private sale to Tommy takes place in early 2016, the county will need to estimate the 2016 taxes on Parcel A because neither it nor the city would have finalized its tax rates for the 2016–2017 tax year. Tommy would need to be informed that, depending on the tax rates adopted by the two local governments, he later may owe additional taxes for the 2016 tax year or may be entitled to a refund of some of the estimated 2016 taxes he pays at the private sale.

E. Input from Other Local Governments?

The local government that purchases the property at the tax foreclosure has the authority to decide what to do with the property without consulting other local governments that previously had liens on the property. Those other local governments have a right to share in the proceeds of any subsequent sale, but they have no right to decide if, when, or how that sale occurs.

In the example in section XIV.D, above, Carolina County has the discretion to hold or sell Parcel A without input from Blue Devil City. If the county decides to sell the property, it alone may determine the appropriate method of sale without input from Blue Devil City. If after the sale the city thinks the county did a poor job of maximizing the property's sale price, the city will have very little recourse.[138] If the city wants to have input in the sale process, it needs to purchase the property itself or jointly with the county at the foreclosure sale.

F. Distribution of Sale Proceeds

Regardless of the sale method, if a local government sells property it purchased at a tax foreclosure it must share the proceeds of that sale with other local governments that had liens on the property.[139]

All taxes, interest, and costs have the same payment priority regardless of which year they arose or which government levied the taxes.[140] This amount must include taxes that would have become liens on the property as of the most recent January 1 were the property not owned by the local government as a result of its purchase at the foreclosure sale.[141] If the sale does not produce enough cash to pay off all of these taxes, interest, and costs, they must be satisfied pro-rata based on the percentage of the total owed to each government. Special assessments are paid after taxes, interest, and costs.

Here is an example: Assume Carolina County purchased Parcel C at its foreclosure sale in November 2014. At the time, $10,000 in taxes, interest, costs, and special assessments were owed on the property. $6,000 of that amount was owed to the county. $4,000 was owed to Blue Devil City, including $2,000 in special assessments.

Carolina County decides to sell the property at a public sale in February 2015. The 2015 taxes on Parcel C would have become a lien on the property as of January 1, 2015, were it not owned by the county on that date. G.S. 105-376(b) requires the county to include these new taxes in the distribution calculation. The 2015 taxes will need to be estimated if the county and city have yet to set their tax rates at the time of sale. For this example, assume that the estimated 2015 taxes on Parcel C are $3,000 for the county and $1,000 for the city.

In sum, the county holds Parcel C for the benefit of itself and the city for $14,000: $9,000 in taxes, interest, and costs owed the county, $3,000 in taxes interest, and costs owed to the city, and $2,000 in special assessments owed to the city.

---

138. The city could sue the county and allege that by selling the property at far below market value the county failed to satisfy its obligations to hold the property for the benefit of other local governments that had tax liens on the property. But such a lawsuit is unlikely to be worth the time and expense involved.

139. G.S. 105-376(b).

140. G.S. 105-356(a).

141. G.S. 105-376(b). Note that in the unlikely case where the purchasing government uses the property for a public use prior to selling the property, then the taxes for those years should not be included in the distribution calculation.

Assume the county sells Parcel C for $8,000. There is not enough cash from this sale to pay off all of the $14,000 owed on the property, meaning that some of those debts will not be paid. The sections below show how these sale proceeds should be distributed.[142]

1. Property Taxes, Interest, and Costs

Including the post-foreclosure taxes, a total of $12,000 in taxes, interest, and related costs are owed on the property. Because the sale produced only $8,000, these taxes must be paid pro-rata. The county accounts for 75 percent of the total ($9,000/$12,000), while the city accounts for 25 percent ($3,000/$12,000). It follows that the county should receive 75 percent of the sale proceeds, or $6,000. The city should receive the remaining $2,000.

2. Special Assessments

There are no sale proceeds remaining to pay the special assessments, which are second in priority and paid after property taxes, interest, and costs.

3. Surplus Proceeds

In this example, there are not enough sale proceeds to satisfy all of the debts on the property, much less any surplus. What if the local government were able to sell the purchased property for more than the amounts owed on it? In that happy scenario, the local government that sells the property may keep the excess cash and use it for any legal public purpose.[143]

XV. Post-Foreclosure Issues

A. Status of Tax Liens on the Property

Property sold at a tax foreclosure must be sold free and clear of liens for all taxes and other obligations included in the foreclosure judgment.[144] This fact remains true regardless of whether the property is sold to a third party or to a local government. But the foreclosure property could be subject to a tax lien for the coming fiscal year if that lien was not included in the foreclosure.

For example, assume that a county dockets an *in rem* judgment in November 2015 and sells the property in March 2015. The 2015 taxes would not have been included in the judgment because they were not yet a lien on the property at the time the judgment was docketed. Whoever buys the property will take it subject to the 2015 tax lien.

The lien for the coming fiscal tax year will also remain on the property in the hands of the new owner if a local government buys the property at the initial foreclosure sale and later sells it to a third party. Consider the example in section XIV.F, above, of Carolina County selling Parcel C after buying the property at its own foreclosure. The county received $6,000 as payment for property taxes,

---

142. This example assumes that the county did not incur any additional costs (advertising, sheriff's fees, etc.) when selling the property. If it did, those costs would be paid first, then the remaining amounts would be shared with the county and the city pro-rata.

143. Note that this is not the case when the original foreclosure sale produces surplus proceeds.

144. G.S. 105-375(i) ("[t]he purchaser . . . shall acquire title to the property in fee simple free and clear of all claims, rights, interests, and liens except the liens of other taxes or special assessments not paid from the purchase price and not included in the judgment.")

interest, and costs, while the city received $2,000. All of that amount should be applied to the old taxes that were included in the foreclosure.[145] No funds remain to pay off the (estimated) 2015 taxes on Parcel C. This means that the buyer would take Parcel C subject to the lien for the full amount of county and city 2015 taxes.

Prior to accepting bids for foreclosure property, local governments must make clear to all potential buyers about the existence of any liens for the coming property tax year.

B. Unpaid Taxes

Because property is sold free and clear of all liens included in the foreclosure judgment, the local government has no more remedies against that property to satisfy those taxes. The government also loses all collection remedies against the taxpayer's *personal* property once a foreclosure action begins.[146] These two facts combine to eliminate all Machinery Act collection remedies for taxes included in a foreclosure judgment, even if the foreclosure sale does not produce enough funds to satisfy those taxes.[147]

The only collection remedy for taxes that remain unpaid after a foreclosure is the set-off debt collection process aimed at taxpayers' state income tax refunds.[148] However, the success of that remedy is far from guaranteed. If the taxpayer never receives a state income tax refund from North Carolina, the local government will be out of luck. The same is true if the taxpayer is not an individual. Although the set-off debt collection statute authorizes its use against corporations, as of 2015 the clearinghouse that processes the requests had not developed procedures for use against any taxpayers other than individual taxpayers.[149]

As a result, most local governments will want to "write off" unpaid taxes following a foreclosure. Technically, the only way to accomplish this goal is through the insolvents list described in the Machinery Act's settlement provisions.[150]

Following a foreclosure, the tax collector may ask the governing board to add any unpaid taxes owed on the foreclosed property to the insolvents list. Once those taxes are at least five years past due, the tax collector may ask the governing board to relieve him or her of the charge for those taxes.[151]

---

145. *See* Chris McLaughlin, *Allocating Tax Payments*, Coates' Canons: NC Local Gov't L. Blog (UNC School of Government, Apr. 23, 2015), http://canons.sog.unc.edu/?p=8077.

146. G.S. 105-366(b) authorizes attachment and garnishment or levy and sale against personal property at any time between the date the taxes become delinquent and the date on which a foreclosure complaint is filed under G.S. 105-374 or a judgment is docketed under G.S. 105-375.

147. This section refers to unpaid taxes that were included in the foreclosure judgment. New taxes that became a lien on the property since the docketing of that judgment remain fully collectible unless they are satisfied with the proceeds of a post-foreclosure sale by a local government who purchased the property at the original foreclosure sale. See section XIV, above, for more on the obligations of a local government that purchases property at a foreclosure sale.

148. G.S. Ch. 105A.

149. See the website of the North Carolina Local Government Debt Setoff Clearinghouse: www.ncsetoff.org/.

150. G.S. 105-373(a)(2) and (g). That said, many and perhaps even most local governments do not use the insolvents list procedure. Instead, each year the governing board adopts a resolution eliminating the obligation of the tax collector to collect all taxes that are more than ten years past due. While this straightforward approach is understandably attractive, it is not authorized by the Machinery Act.

151. The governing board must charge the tax collector with responsibility for each year's taxes. G.S. 105-321. This charge creates the tax collector's obligation and authority to use all lawful collection methods to collect that year's taxes. This obligation remains in effect unless and until the governing board eliminates it for taxes that have been added to the insolvents list and are more than five years past due.

After that occurs, the tax collector no longer has the obligation to collect these taxes. They need not be included on any future settlements or similar reports by the collector to the board.

C. Subsequent Legal Challenges

Taxpayers who believe their property was sold improperly by a local government under the tax foreclosure provisions may have their claims heard in court even after a sale is confirmed. Most often, those challenges will be based on the local government's alleged failure to provide adequate notice.[152] G.S. 105-377 creates a one-year limitation on a challenge to the validity of title to real property. However, that limitation applies to limited situations in which a party claims that the title it holds to the property in question is superior to that purchased by the high bidder at a foreclosure sale.[153] The one-year limitation does not apply to legal claims that allege defects in the foreclosure process, such as lack of notice.[154]

---

152. See the cases listed in note 2, above.

153. See, for example, *Overstreet v. City of Raleigh*, 75 N.C. App. 351 (1984), in which a claim of title by adverse possession to property sold at foreclosure was barred by the one-year limitation on challenges to title.

154. *See* Bd. of Cty. Comm'rs v. Bumpass, 233 N.C. 190 (1951), Henderson v. Osteen, 292 N.C. 692 (1977), *and* Howell v. Treece, 70 N.C. App. 322 (1984).

Appendix

North Carolina Statutes (G.S.) Relevant to the *In Rem* Foreclosure Process

G.S. Chapter 7A, Subchapter VI, Article 28, Uniform Costs and Fees in the Trial Divisions
§ 7A-311. Uniform civil process fees.

(a)   In a civil action or special proceeding, except for actions brought under Chapter 50B of the General Statutes, the following fees and commissions shall be assessed, collected, and remitted to the county:

(1)   a.   For each item of civil process served, including summons, subpoenas, notices, motions, orders, writs and pleadings, the sum of thirty dollars ($30.00). When two or more items of civil process are served simultaneously on one party, only one thirty-dollar ($30.00) fee shall be charged.

b.   When an item of civil process is served on two or more persons or organizations, a separate service charge shall be made for each person or organization. The process fee shall be remitted to the county. This subsection shall not apply to service of summons to jurors.

c.   At least fifty percent (50%) of the fees collected pursuant to this subdivision shall be used by the county to ensure the timely service of process within the county, which may include the hiring of additional law enforcement personnel upon the recommendation of the sheriff.

(2)   For the seizure of personal property and its care after seizure, all necessary expenses, in addition to any fees for service of process.

(3)   For all sales by the sheriff of property, either real or personal, or for funds collected by the sheriff under any judgment, five percent (5%) on the first five hundred dollars ($500.00), and two and one-half percent (2 ½%) on all sums over five hundred dollars ($500.00), plus necessary expenses of sale. Whenever an execution is issued to the sheriff, and subsequently while the execution is in force and outstanding, and after the sheriff has served or attempted to serve such execution, the judgment, or any part thereof, is paid directly or indirectly to the judgment creditor, the fee herein is payable to the sheriff on the amount so paid. The judgment creditor shall be responsible for collecting and paying all execution fees on amounts paid directly to the judgment creditor.

(4)   For execution of a judgment of ejectment, all necessary expenses, in addition to any fees for service of process.

(5)   For necessary transportation of individuals to or from State institutions or another state, the same mileage and subsistence allowances as are provided for State employees.

(b)   All fees that are required to be assessed, collected, and remitted under subsection (a) of this section shall be collected in advance (except in suits in forma pauperis) except those contingent on expenses or sales prices. When the fee is not collected in advance or at the time of assessment, a lien shall exist in favor of the county on all property of the party owing the fee. If the fee remains unpaid it shall be entered as a judgment against the debtor and shall be docketed in the judgment docket in the office of the clerk of superior court.

(c)   The process fees and commissions set forth in this section are complete and exclusive and in lieu of any and all other process fees and commissions in civil actions and special proceedings.

G.S. Chapter 105, Subchapter II, Article 26, Collection and Foreclosure of Taxes
§ 105-356. Priority of tax liens.

(a)   On Real Property. - The lien of taxes imposed on real and personal property shall attach to real property at the time prescribed in G.S. 105-355(a). The priority of that lien shall be determined in accordance with the following rules:

(1)   Subject to the provisions of the Revenue Act prescribing the priority of the lien for State taxes, the lien of taxes imposed under the provisions of this Subchapter shall be superior to all other liens, assessments, charges, rights, and claims of any and every kind in and to the real property to which the lien for taxes

attaches regardless of the claimant and regardless of whether acquired prior or subsequent to the attachment of the lien for taxes.

(2) The liens of taxes of all taxing units shall be of equal dignity.

(3) The priority of the lien for taxes shall not be affected by transfer of title to the real property after the lien has attached, nor shall it be affected by the death, receivership, or bankruptcy of the owner of the real property to which the lien attaches.

(b) On Personal Property. - The lien of taxes on real and personal property shall attach to personal property at the time prescribed in G.S. 105-355(b). The priority of that lien shall be determined in accordance with the following rules:

(1) The tax lien, when it attaches to personal property, shall, insofar as it represents taxes imposed upon the property to which the lien attaches, be superior to all other liens and rights whether such other liens and rights are prior or subsequent to the tax lien in point of time.

(2) The tax lien, when it attaches to personal property, shall, insofar as it represents taxes imposed upon property other than that to which the lien attaches, be inferior to prior valid liens and perfected security interests and superior to all subsequent liens and security interests.

(3) As between the tax liens of different taxing units, the tax lien first attaching shall be superior.

§ 105-369. Advertisement of tax liens on real property for failure to pay taxes.

(a) Report of Unpaid Taxes That Are Liens on Real Property. - In February of each year, the tax collector must report to the governing body the total amount of unpaid taxes for the current fiscal year that are liens on real property. A county tax collector's report is due the first Monday in February, and a municipal tax collector's report is due the second Monday in February. Upon receipt of the report, the governing body must order the tax collector to advertise the tax liens. For purposes of this section, district taxes collected by county tax collectors shall be regarded as county taxes and district taxes collected by municipal tax collectors shall be regarded as municipal taxes.

(b) Repealed by Session Laws 1983 (Regular Session, 1984), c. 1013.

(b1) Notice to Owner. - After the governing body orders the tax collector to advertise the tax liens, the tax collector must send a notice to the record owner of each affected parcel of property, as determined as of the date the taxes became delinquent. The notice must be sent to the owner's last known address by first-class mail at least 30 days before the date the advertisement is to be published. The notice must state the principal amount of unpaid taxes that are a lien on the parcel to be advertised and inform the owner that the name of the record owner as of the date the taxes became delinquent will appear in a newspaper advertisement of delinquent taxes if the taxes are not paid before the publication date. Failure to mail the notice required by this section to the correct record owner does not affect the validity of the tax lien or of any foreclosure action.

(c) Time and Contents of Advertisement. - A tax collector's failure to comply with this subsection does not affect the validity of the taxes or tax liens. The county tax collector shall advertise county tax liens by posting a notice of the liens at the county courthouse and by publishing each lien at least one time in one or more newspapers having general circulation in the taxing unit. The municipal tax collector shall advertise municipal tax liens by posting a notice of the liens at the city or town hall and by publishing each lien at least one time in one or more newspapers having general circulation in the taxing unit. Advertisements of tax liens shall be made during the period March 1 through June 30. The costs of newspaper advertising shall be paid by the taxing unit. If the taxes of two or more taxing units are collected by the same tax collector, the tax liens of each unit shall be advertised separately unless, under the provisions of a special act or contractual agreement between the taxing units, joint advertisement is permitted.

The posted notice and newspaper advertisement shall set forth the following information:

(1) Repealed by Session Laws 2006-106, s. 2, effective for taxes imposed for taxable years beginning on or after July 1, 2006.

(1a) The name of the record owner as of the date the taxes became delinquent for each parcel on which the taxing unit has a lien for unpaid taxes, in alphabetical order.

(1b) After the information required by subdivision (1a) of this subsection for each parcel, a brief description of each parcel of land to which a lien has attached and a statement of the principal amount of the taxes constituting a lien against the parcel.

(2) A statement that the amounts advertised will be increased by interest and costs and that the omission of interest and costs from the amounts advertised will not constitute waiver of the taxing unit's claim for those items.

(3) In the event the list of tax liens has been divided for purposes of advertisement in more than one newspaper, a statement of the names of all newspapers in which advertisements will appear and the dates on which they will be published.

(4) A statement that the taxing unit may foreclose the tax liens and sell the real property subject to the liens in satisfaction of its claim for taxes.

(d)   Costs. - Each parcel of real property advertised pursuant to this section shall be assessed an advertising fee to cover the actual cost of the advertisement. Actual advertising costs per parcel shall be determined by the tax collector on any reasonable basis. Advertising costs assessed pursuant to this subsection are taxes.

(e)   Payments during Advertising Period. - At any time during the advertisement period, any parcel may be withdrawn from the list by payment of the taxes plus interest that has accrued to the time of payment and a proportionate part of the advertising fee to be determined by the tax collector. Thereafter, the tax collector shall delete that parcel from any subsequent advertisement, but the tax collector is not liable for failure to make the deletion.

(f)   Listing and Advertising in Wrong Name. - No tax lien is void because the real property to which the lien attached was listed or advertised in the name of a person other than the person in whose name the property should have been listed for taxation if the property was in other respects correctly described on the abstract or in the advertisement.

(g)   Wrongful Advertisement. - Any tax collector or deputy tax collector who willfully advertises any tax lien knowing that the property is not subject to taxation or that the taxes advertised have been paid is guilty of a Class 3 misdemeanor, and shall be required to pay the injured party all damages sustained in consequence.

§ 105-375. In rem method of foreclosure.

(a)   Intent of Section. - It is hereby declared to be the intention of this section that proceedings brought under it shall be strictly in rem. It is further declared to be the intention of this section to provide, as an alternative to G.S. 105-374, a simple and inexpensive method of enforcing payment of taxes necessarily levied, to the knowledge of all persons, for the requirements of local governments in this State; and to recognize, in authorizing this proceeding, that all persons owning interests in real property know or should know that the tax lien on their real property may be foreclosed and the property sold for failure to pay taxes.

(b)   Docketing Certificate of Taxes as Judgment. - In lieu of following the procedure set forth in G.S. 105-374, the governing body of any taxing unit may direct the tax collector to file with the clerk of superior court, no earlier than 30 days after the tax liens were advertised, a certificate showing the following: the name of the taxpayer as defined in G.S. 105-273(17), for each parcel on which the taxing unit has a lien for unpaid taxes, together with the amount of taxes, penalties, interest, and costs that are a lien thereon; the year or years for which the taxes are due; and a description of the property sufficient to permit its identification by parol testimony. The fees for docketing and indexing the certificate shall be payable to the clerk of superior court at the time the taxes are collected or the property is sold.

(c)   Notice to Taxpayer and Others. -
   (1)   Notice required. - The tax collector filing the certificate provided for in subsection (b) of this section, shall, at least 30 days prior to docketing the judgment, send notice of the tax lien foreclosure to the taxpayer, as defined in G.S. 105-273(17), at the taxpayer's last known address, and to all lienholders of record who have a lien against the taxpayer (including any liens referred to in the conveyance of the property to the taxpayer).
   (2)   Contents of notice. - All notice required by this subsection shall state that a judgment will be docketed and the proposed date of the docketing, that execution will be issued as provided by law, a brief description of the real property affected, and that the lien may be satisfied prior to judgment being entered.
   (3)   Service of notice. - The notice required by this subsection shall be sent to the taxpayer by registered or certified mail, return receipt requested.
   (4)   Additional efforts may be required. - If within 10 days following the mailing of the notice, a return receipt has not been received by the tax collector indicating receipt of the notice, then the tax collector shall do both of the following:
      a.   Make reasonable efforts to locate and notify the taxpayer and all lienholders of record prior to the docketing of the judgment and the issuance of the execution. Reasonable efforts may include posting the notice in a conspicuous place on the property, or, if the property has an address to which mail may be delivered, mailing the notice by first-class mail to the attention of the occupant.
      b.   Have a notice published in a newspaper of general circulation in the county once a week for two consecutive weeks directed to, and naming, all unnotified lienholders and the taxpayer that a judgment will be docketed against the taxpayer.
   (5)   Costs of notice added to lien. - All costs of mailing and publication, plus a charge of two hundred fifty dollars ($250.00) to defray administrative costs, shall be added to the amount of taxes that are a lien on the real property and shall be paid by the taxpayer to the taxing unit at the time the taxes are collected or the property is sold.

(d)   Effect of Docketing Certificate of Taxes Due. - Immediately upon the docketing and indexing of a certificate as provided in subsection (b), above, the taxes, penalties, interest, and costs shall constitute a valid judgment against the real property described therein, with the priority provided for tax liens in G.S. 105-356. The judgment, except as expressly provided in this section, shall have the same force and effect as a duly rendered judgment of the superior court directing sale of the property for the satisfaction of the tax lien, and it shall bear interest at an annual rate of eight percent (8%).

(e)   Special Assessments. - Street, sidewalk, and other special assessments may be included in any judgment for taxes taken under this section, or the special assessments may be included in a separate judgment docketed under this section. The tax collector may use such a judgment as a method of foreclosing the lien of special assessments. When used to foreclose the lien of special assessments, the procedure may be instituted at any time after the assessment or installment falls due and remains unpaid; the waiting period required by subsection (b) of this section does not apply to the foreclosure of special assessments.

(f)   Motion to Set Aside. - At any time prior to the issuance of execution, any person having an interest in the real property to be foreclosed may appear before the clerk of superior court and move to set aside the judgment on the ground that the tax has been paid or that the tax lien on which the judgment is based is invalid.

(g)   Cancellation upon Payment. - Upon payment in full of any judgment docketed under this section, together with interest thereon and costs accrued to the date of payment, the tax collector receiving payment shall certify the fact thereof to the clerk of superior court and cancel the judgment.

(h)   Relationship between G.S. 105-374 and This Section. - If, before the issuance of execution on the judgment under subsection (i), below, the taxing unit is made a defendant in a foreclosure action brought against the property under G.S. 105-374, it shall file an answer in that proceeding and thereafter all proceedings shall be governed by order of the court in accordance with that section.

(i)   Issuance of Execution. - At any time after three months and before two years from the indexing of the judgment as provided in subsection (b), above, execution shall be issued at the request of the tax collector in the same manner as executions are issued upon other judgments of the superior court, and the real property shall be sold by the sheriff in the same manner as other real property is sold under execution with the following exceptions:

(1)   No debtor's exemption shall be allowed.

(2)   In lieu of personal service of notice on the taxpayer, the sheriff shall send notice by registered or certified mail, return receipt requested, to the taxpayer at the taxpayer's last known address at least 30 days prior to the day fixed for the sale. If within 10 days following the mailing of the notice, a return receipt has not been received by the sheriff indicating receipt of the notice, then the sheriff shall make additional efforts to locate and notify the taxpayer and all lienholders of record of the sale under execution in accordance with subdivision (4) of subsection (c) of this section.

(3)   The sheriff shall add to the amount of the judgment as costs of the sale any postage expenses incurred by the tax collector and the sheriff in foreclosing under this section.

(4)   In any advertisement or posted notice of sale under execution, the sheriff may (and at the request of the governing body shall) combine the advertisements or notices for properties to be sold under executions against the properties of different taxpayers in favor of the same taxing unit or group of units; however, the property included in each judgment shall be separately described and the name of the taxpayer specified in connection with each.

The purchaser at the execution sale shall acquire title to the property in fee simple free and clear of all claims, rights, interests, and liens except the liens of other taxes or special assessments not paid from the purchase price and not included in the judgment.

(j)   Attorney's Fee. - The governing body of the taxing unit may make whatever arrangement it deems satisfactory for compensating an attorney rendering assistance or advice in foreclosure proceedings brought under this section, but the attorney's fee shall not be added to the judgment as part of the costs of the action.

(k)   Consolidation of Liens. - By agreement between the governing bodies, two or more taxing units may consolidate their tax liens for the purpose of docketing a judgment, or may have one execution issued for separate judgments, against the same property. In like manner, one execution may issue for separate judgments in favor of one or more taxing units against the same property for different years' taxes.

(l)   Purchase and Resale by Taxing Unit. - The rights of a taxing unit to purchase real property at a foreclosure sale and resell it are governed by G.S. 105-376.

(m)   Procedure if Section Declared Unconstitutional. - If any provisions of this section are declared invalid or unconstitutional by the Supreme Court of North Carolina, a United States district court of three judges, the United States Circuit Court of Appeals, or the United States Supreme Court, all taxing units that have proceeded under this section shall have five years from the date of the filing of the opinion (or, in the case of appeal, from the date of the filing of the opinion on appeal) in which to institute foreclosure actions under G.S. 105-374 for all taxes included in judgments taken under this section and for subsequent taxes due or which, but for purchase of the property by the taxing unit, would have become due; and such judicial decision shall not have the effect of invalidating the tax lien or disturbing its priority.

§ 105-376. Taxing unit as purchaser at foreclosure sale; payment of purchase price; resale of property acquired by taxing unit.

(a)   Taxing Unit as Purchaser. - Any taxing unit (or two or more taxing units jointly) may bid at a foreclosure sale conducted under G.S. 105-374 or G.S. 105-375, and any taxing unit that becomes the successful bidder may assign its bid at any time by private sale for not less than the amount of the bid.

(b)   Payment of Purchase Price by Taxing Units; Status of Property Purchased by Taxing Units. - Any taxing unit that becomes the purchaser at a tax foreclosure sale may, in the discretion of its governing body, pay only that part of the purchase price that would not be distributed to it and other taxing units on account of taxes, penalties, interest, and such costs as accrued prior to the initiation of the foreclosure action under G.S. 105-374 or docketing of a judgment under G.S. 105-375. Thereafter, in such a case, the purchasing taxing unit shall hold the property for the benefit of all taxing units that have an interest in the property as defined in this subsection (b). All net income from real property so acquired and the proceeds thereof, when resold, shall be first used to reimburse the purchasing unit for disbursements actually made by it in connection with the foreclosure action and the purchase of the property, and any balance remaining shall be distributed to the taxing units having an interest therein in proportion to their interests. The total interest of each taxing unit, including the purchasing unit, shall be determined by adding:

(1)   The taxes of the unit, with penalties, interest, and costs (other than costs already reimbursed to the purchasing unit) to satisfy which the property was ordered sold;

(2)   Other taxes of the unit, with penalties, interest, and costs which would have been paid in full from the purchase price had the purchase price been paid in full;

(3)   Taxes of the unit, with penalties, interest, and costs to which the foreclosure sale was made subject; and

(4)   The principal amount of all taxes which became liens on the property after purchase at the foreclosure sale or which would have become liens thereon but for the purchase, but no amount shall be included for taxes for years in which (on the day as of which property was to be listed for taxation) the property was being used by the purchasing unit for a public purpose.

If the amount of net income and proceeds of resale distributable exceeds the total interests of all taxing units defined in this subsection (b), the remainder shall be applied to any special benefit assessments to satisfy which the sale was ordered or to which the sale was made subject, and any balance remaining shall accrue to the purchasing unit.

When any real property that has been purchased as provided in this section is permanently dedicated to use for a public purpose, the purchasing unit shall make settlement with other taxing units having an interest in the property (as defined in this subsection) in such manner and in such amount as may be agreed upon by the governing bodies; and if no agreement can be reached, the amount to be paid shall be determined by a resident judge of the superior court in the district in which the property is situated.

Nothing in this section shall be construed as requiring the purchasing unit to secure the approval of other interested taxing units before reselling the property or as requiring the purchasing unit to pay other interested taxing units in full if the net income and resale price are insufficient to make such payments.

Any taxing unit purchasing property at a foreclosure sale may, in the discretion of its governing body, instead of following the foregoing provisions of this section, make full payment of the purchase price, and thereafter it shall hold the property as sole owner in the same manner as it holds other real property, subject only to taxes and special assessments, with penalties, interest, and costs, to which the sale was made subject.

(c)   Resale of Real Property Purchased by Taxing Units. - Real property purchased at a tax foreclosure sale by a taxing unit may be resold at any time (for such price as the governing body of the taxing unit may approve) at a sale conducted in the manner provided by law for sales of other real property of the taxing unit. However, a purchasing taxing unit, in the discretion of its governing body, may resell such property to the former owner or to any other person formerly having an interest in the property at private sale for an amount not less than the taxing unit's interest therein if it holds the property as sole owner or for an amount not less than the total interests of all taxing units (other than special assessments due the taxing unit holding title) if it holds the property for the benefit of all such units.

§ 105-377. Time for contesting validity of tax foreclosure title.

Notwithstanding any other provisions of law prescribing the period for commencing an action, no action or proceeding shall be brought to contest the validity of any title to real property acquired by a taxing unit or by a private purchaser in any tax foreclosure action or proceeding authorized by this Subchapter or by other laws of this State in force at the time the title was acquired, nor shall any motion to reopen or set aside the judgment in any such tax foreclosure action or proceeding be entertained after one year from the date on which the deed is recorded.

§ 105-378. Limitation on use of remedies.

(a)   Use of Remedies Barred. - No county or municipality may maintain an action or procedure to enforce any remedy provided by law for the collection of taxes or the enforcement of any tax liens (whether the taxes or tax liens are evidenced by the original tax receipts, tax sales certificates, or otherwise) unless the action or procedure is instituted within 10 years from the date the taxes became due.

(b)   Not Applicable to Special Assessments. - The provisions of subsection (a), above, shall not be construed to apply to the lien of special assessments.

(c)   Repealed by Session Laws 1998-98, s. 26, effective August 14, 1998.

(d)   Enforcement and Collection Delayed Pending Appeal. - When the board of county commissioners or municipal governing body delivers a tax receipt to a tax collector for any assessment that has been or is subsequently appealed to the county board of equalization and review or the Property Tax Commission, the tax collector may not seek collection of taxes or enforcement of a tax lien resulting from the assessment until the appeal has been finally adjudicated. The tax collector, however, may send an initial bill or notice to the taxpayer.

G.S. Chapter 1, Subchapter X, Article 29B, Execution Sales, Part 1, General Provisions

§ 1-339.41. Definitions.

(a)   An execution sale is a sale of property by a sheriff or other officer made pursuant to an execution.

(b)   As used in this article,

    (1)   "Sale" means an execution sale;

    (2)   "Sheriff" means a sheriff or any officer authorized to hold an execution sale.

§ 1-339.42. Clerk's authority to fix procedural details.

The clerk of the superior court who issues an execution has authority to fix and determine all necessary procedural details with respect to sales in all instances in which this Article fails to make definite provisions as to such procedure.

§ 1-339.43. Days on which sale may be held.

A sale may be held on any day except Sunday.

§ 1-339.44. Place of sale.

(a)   Every sale of real property shall be held at the courthouse door in the county where the property is situated unless the property consists of a single tract situated in two or more counties.

(b)   A sale of a single tract of real property situated in two or more counties may be held at the courthouse door in any one of the counties in which any part of the tract is situated, but no sheriff shall hold any sale outside his own county. As used in this section, a "single tract" means any tract which has a continuous boundary, regardless of whether parts thereof may have been acquired at different times or from different persons or whether it may have been subdivided into other units or lots, or whether it is sold as a whole or in parts.

(c)   A sale of personal property may be held at any place in his county designated by the sheriff in the notice of sale.

§ 1-339.45. Presence of personal property at sale required.

A sheriff holding a sale of personal property shall have the property present at the place of sale.

§ 1-339.46. Sale as a whole or in parts.

When real property to be sold consists of separate lots or other units or when personal property consists of more than one article, the sheriff may sell such real or personal property as a whole or in designated parts, or may offer the property for sale by each method, and then sell the property by the method which produces the highest price; but regardless of which method is followed, the sheriff shall not sell more property than is reasonably necessary to satisfy the judgment together with the costs of the execution and the sale.

§ 1-339.47. Sale to be made for cash.

Every sale shall be made for cash.

§ 1-339.48. Life of execution.

If an execution is issued on a judgment, within the time provided by G.S. 1-306, and a sale, by authority of that execution, is commenced within the time provided by G.S. 1-310, the sale, including any resale, may be had and completed even though such sales, resales or other procedure are had after the time when the execution is required to be returned by

G.S. 1-310, or after the time within which an execution could be issued with respect to such judgment pursuant to the provisions of G.S. 1-306. For the purpose of this section, a sale is commenced when the notice of sale is first published in the case of real property as required by G.S. 1-339.52, or first posted in the case of personal property as required by G.S. 1-339.53.

§ 1-339.49. Penalty for selling contrary to law.

A sheriff or other officer who makes any sale contrary to the true intent and meaning of this Article shall forfeit two hundred dollars to any person suing for it, one half for his own use and the other half to the use of the county where the offense is committed.

§ 1-339.50. Officer's return of no sale for want of bidders; penalty.

When a sheriff or other officer returns upon an execution that he has made no sale for want of bidders, he must state in his return the several places he has advertised and offered for sale the property levied on; and an officer failing to make such statement is on motion subject to a fine of forty dollars, for the use and benefit of the plaintiff in the execution; for which, on motion of the plaintiff, judgment shall be granted by the court to which, or by justice to whom, the execution shall be returned. Nothing in, nor any recovery under, this section is a bar to any action for a false return against the sheriff or other officer.

G.S. Chapter 1, Subchapter X, Article 29B, Execution Sales, Part 2, Procedure for Sale
§ 1-339.51. Contents of notice of sale.

The notice of sale shall
   (1)   Refer to the execution authorizing the sale;
   (2)   Designate the date, hour and place of sale;
   (3)   Describe real property to be sold, by reference or otherwise, sufficiently to identify it, and may add such further description as will acquaint bidders with the nature and location of the property;
   (4)   Describe personal property to be sold sufficiently to indicate its nature and quantity, and may add such further description as will acquaint bidders with the nature of the property; and
   (5)   State that the sale will be made to the highest bidder for cash.

§ 1-339.52. Posting and publishing notice of sale of real property.

(a)   The notice of sale of real property shall:
   (1)   Be posted, in the area designated by the clerk of superior court for the posting of notices in the county in which the property is situated, for at least 20 days immediately preceding the sale; and
   (2)   Be published once a week for at least two successive weeks:
      a.   In a newspaper qualified for legal advertising published in the county; or
      b.   If no newspaper qualified for legal advertising is published in the county, in a newspaper having general circulation in the county.
(b)   When the notice of sale is published in a newspaper:
   (1)   The period from the date of the first publication to the date of the last publication, both dates inclusive, shall not be less than seven days, including Sundays; and
   (2)   The date of the last publication shall be not more than 10 days preceding the date of the sale.
(c)   When the real property to be sold is situated in more than one county, the provisions of subsections (a) and (b) shall be complied with in each county in which any part of the property is situated.

§ 1-339.53. Posting notice of sale of personal property.

The notice of sale of personal property, except in the case of perishable property as specified in G.S. 1-339.56, shall be posted, in the area designated by the clerk of superior court for the posting of notices in the county in which the sale is to be held, for 10 days immediately preceding the date of sale.

§ 1-339.54. Notice to judgment debtor of sale of real property.

In addition to complying with G.S. 1-339.52, relating to posting and publishing the notice of sale, the sheriff shall, at least ten days before the sale of real property,
   (1)   If the judgment debtor is found in the county, serve a copy of the notice of sale on him personally, or
   (2)   If the judgment debtor is not found in the county,

a. Send a copy of the notice of sale by registered mail to the judgment debtor at his last address known to the sheriff, and

b. Serve a copy of the notice of sale on the judgment debtor's agent, if there is in the county a person known to the sheriff to be an agent who has custody or management of, or who exercises control over, any property in the county belonging to the judgment debtor.

§ 1-339.55. Notification of Governor and Attorney General.

When the State is a stockholder in any corporation whose property is to be sold under execution, notice in writing shall be given by the sheriff by registered mail to the Governor and the Attorney General at least thirty days before the sale, stating the time and place of the sale and including a copy of the process under the authority of which such sale is to be made. Any sale held without complying with the provisions of this section is invalid with respect to the State.

§ 1-339.56. Exception; perishable property.

If, in the opinion of the sheriff, any personal property levied on under execution is perishable because subject to rapid deterioration, he shall forthwith report such levy, together with a description of the property, to the clerk of the superior court, and request instructions as to the sale of such property. If the clerk then determines that the property is such perishable property, he shall thereupon order a sale thereof to be held at such time and place and upon such notice to be given in such manner and for such length of time as he deems advisable. If the clerk determines that the property is not perishable, he shall order it to be sold in the same manner as other nonperishable property.

§ 1-339.57. Satisfaction of judgment before sale completed.

If, prior to the time fixed for a sale, or prior to the expiration of the time allowed for submitting any upset bid, payment is made or tendered to the sheriff of the judgment and costs with respect to which the execution was issued, and the sheriff's fees, commissions and expenses which have accrued, together with any expenses incurred on account of the sale or proposed sale including costs incurred in caring for the property levied on, then any right to effect a sale pursuant to the execution ceases.

§ 1-339.58. Postponement of sale.

(a) The sheriff may postpone the sale to a day certain not later than six days, exclusive of Sunday, after the original date for the sale:

(1) When there are no bidders,

(2) When, in the sheriff's judgment, the number of prospective bidders at the sale is substantially decreased by inclement weather or by any casualty,

(3) When there are so many other sales advertised to be held at the same time and place as to make it inexpedient and impracticable, in the sheriff's judgment, to hold the sale on that day,

(4) When the sheriff is unable to hold the sale because of illness or for other good reason, or

(5) When other good cause exists.

(b) Upon postponement of a sale, the sheriff shall:

(1) At the time and place advertised for the sale, publicly announce the postponement of the sale; and

(2) On the same day, attach to or enter on the original notice of sale or a copy of the notice, posted as provided by G.S. 1-339.52 in the case of real property or G.S. 1-339.53 in the case of personal property, a notice of the postponement.

(c) The posted notice of postponement shall:

(1) State that the sale is postponed,

(2) State the hour and date to which the sale is postponed,

(3) State the reason for the postponement, and

(4) Be signed by the sheriff.

(d) If a sale is not held at the time fixed for the sale and is not postponed as provided by this section, or if a postponed sale is not held at the time fixed for the sale, the sheriff shall report the facts with respect thereto to the clerk of the superior court, who shall thereupon make an order for the sale of the property to be held at such time and place and upon such notice to be given in the manner and for the length of time as the clerk of the superior court deems advisable, but nothing in this section relieves the sheriff of liability for the nonperformance of the sheriff's official duty.

§ 1-339.59. Procedure upon dissolution of order restraining or enjoining sale.

(a)   When, before the date fixed for a sale, a judge dissolves an order restraining or enjoining the sale, he may, if the required notice of sale has been given, provide by order that the sale shall be held without additional notice at the time and place originally fixed therefor, or he may, in his discretion, make an order with respect thereto as provided in subsection (b).

(b)   When, after the date fixed for a sale, a judge dissolves an order restraining or enjoining the sale, he shall by order fix the time and place for the sale to be held upon notice to be given in such manner and for such length of time as he deems advisable.

§ 1-339.60. Time of sale.

(a)   A sale shall begin at the time designated in the notice of sale or as soon thereafter as practicable, but not later than one hour after the time fixed therefor unless it is delayed by other sales held at the same place.

(b)   No sale shall commence before 10:00 o'clock A.M. or after 4:00 o'clock P.M.

(c)   No sale shall continue after 4:00 o'clock P.M., except that in cities or towns of more than 5,000 inhabitants, as shown by the most recent federal census, sales of personal property may continue until 10:00 o'clock P.M.

§ 1-339.61. Continuance of uncompleted sale.

A sale commenced but not completed within the time allowed by G.S. 1-339.60 shall be continued by the sheriff to a designated time between 10:00 o'clock A.M. and 4:00 o'clock P.M. the next following day, other than Sunday. In case such continuance becomes necessary, the sheriff shall publicly announce the time to which the sale is continued.

§ 1-339.62. Delivery of personal property; bill of sale.

A sheriff holding a sale of personal property shall deliver the property to the purchaser immediately upon receipt of the purchase price. The sheriff may also execute and deliver a bill of sale or other muniment of title for any personal property sold, and, upon application of the purchaser, shall do so when required by the clerk of the superior court of the county where the property is sold.

§ 1-339.63. Report of sale.

(a)   The sheriff shall, within five days after the date of the sale, file a report thereof with the clerk of the superior court.

(b)   The report shall be signed and shall show

(1)   The title of the action or proceeding;

(2)   The authority under which the sheriff acted;

(3)   The date, hour and place of the sale;

(4)   A description of real property sold, by reference or otherwise, sufficient to identify it, and, if sold in parts, a description of each part so sold;

(5)   A description of personal property sold, sufficient to indicate the nature and quantity of the property sold to each purchaser;

(6)   The name or names of the person or persons to whom the property was sold;

(7)   The price at which the property, or each part thereof, was sold and that such price was the highest bid therefor; and

(8)   The date of the report.

§ 1-339.64. Upset bid on real property; compliance bond.

(a)   An upset bid is an advanced, increased, or raised bid whereby a person offers to purchase real property theretofore sold for an amount exceeding the reported sale price or last upset bid by a minimum of five percent (5%) thereof, but in any event with a minimum increase of seven hundred fifty dollars ($750.00). Subject to the provisions of subsection (b) of this section, an upset bid shall be made by delivering to the clerk of superior court, with whom the report of sale or the last notice of upset bid was filed, a deposit in cash or by certified check or cashier's check satisfactory to the clerk in an amount greater than or equal to five percent (5%) of the amount of the upset bid but in no event less than seven hundred fifty dollars ($750.00). The deposit required by this section shall be filed with the clerk of the superior court, with whom the report of sale or the last notice of upset bid was filed, by the close of normal business hours on the tenth day after the filing of the report of sale or the last notice of upset bid and if the tenth day falls upon a Sunday or legal holiday when the courthouse is closed for transactions, or upon a day in which the office of the clerk is not open for the regular dispatch of its business, the deposit may be made and the notice of upset bid may be filed on the day following when the office is open for the regular dispatch of its business. Except as provided in G.S. 1-339.66A and G.S. 1-339.69, there shall be no resales; however, there may be successive upset bids, each of which shall be followed by a period of 10 days for a further upset bid. If a timely motion for resale is filed under G.S. 1-339.66A, no upset bids may be filed while the motion is pending.

(b)   The clerk of the superior court may require an upset bidder or the highest bidder at a resale held under G.S. 1-339.69 also to deposit with the clerk a cash bond, or, in lieu thereof at the option of the bidder, a surety bond, approved by the clerk. The compliance bond shall be in the amount the clerk deems adequate, but in no case greater than the amount of the bid of the person being required to furnish the bond, less the amount of any required deposit. The compliance bond shall be payable to the State of North Carolina for the use of the parties in interest and shall be conditioned on the principal obligor's compliance with the bid.

(c)   Repealed by Session Laws 2001-271, s. 14, effective January 1, 2002. See editor's note for applicability.

(d)   Repealed by Session Laws 2001-271, s. 14, effective January 1, 2002. See editor's note for applicability.

(e)   At the time that an upset bid on real property is submitted to the court as provided in subsection (a) of this section, together with a compliance bond if one is required, the upset bidder shall file with the clerk a notice of upset bid. The notice of upset bid shall:

(1)   State the name, address, and telephone number of the upset bidder;

(2)   Specify the amount of the upset bid;

(3)   Provide that the sale shall remain open for a period of 10 days after the date on which the notice of upset bid is filed for the filing of additional upset bids as permitted by law; and

(4)   Be signed by the upset bidder or the attorney or the agent of the upset bidder.

(f)   When an upset bid is made as provided in this section, the clerk shall notify the person holding the sale who shall thereafter mail a written notice of upset bid by first-class mail to the last known address of the last prior bidder and the current record owners of the property.

(g)   When an upset bid is made as provided in this section, the last prior bidder, regardless of how the bid was made, is released from any further obligation on account of the bid, and any deposit or bond provided by the last prior bidder shall be released.

(h)   Any person offering to purchase real property by upset bid as permitted in this Article is subject to and bound by the terms of the original notice of sale except as modified by a court order or the provisions of this Article.

(i)   The clerk of superior court shall make all orders as may be just and necessary to safeguard the interests of all parties and may fix and determine all necessary procedural details with respect to upset bids in all instances in which this Article fails to make definite provisions as to that procedure.

§ 1-339.65. Separate upset bids when real property sold in parts; subsequent procedure.

When real property is sold in parts, as provided by G.S. 1-339.46, the sale of any part shall be subject to a separate upset bid; and to the extent the clerk of the superior court having jurisdiction deems advisable, the sale of each part shall thereafter be treated as a separate sale for the purpose of determining the applicable procedure.

§ 1-339.66: Repealed by Session Laws 2001-271, s. 16.

§ 1-339.66A. Ordering resale of real property after upset bid.

Upon motion of an interested person filed within 10 days after a sale or upset bid and for good cause, the clerk of superior court may order a resale of real property when an upset bid is submitted as provided in G.S. 1-339.64. If the motion is granted based on the inadequacy of the last bid, the procedure for the resale is the same in every respect as is provided by this Article in the case of an original public sale, and the last bidder is released from the bidder's obligations under the bid. If the motion is granted for any other reason, the last bid becomes the opening bid at resale, and if there is no bid at resale other than the last bid, the person who made the last bid is the highest bidder at resale. If the motion is denied, the 10-day period for subsequent upset bids begins upon the entry of the order.

§ 1-339.67. Confirmation of sale of real property.

No sale of real property may be consummated until the sale is confirmed by the clerk of the superior court. No order of confirmation may be made until the time for submitting an upset bid, pursuant to G.S. 1-339.64, has expired.

§ 1-339.68. Deed for real property sold; property subject to liens; orders for possession.

(a)   Upon confirmation of a sale of real property, the sheriff, upon order of the clerk of the superior court, shall prepare and tender to the purchaser a duly executed deed for the property sold and, upon compliance by the purchaser with the terms of the sale, shall deliver the deed to the purchaser.

(b)   Any real property sold under execution remains subject to all liens which became effective prior to the lien of the judgment pursuant to which the sale is held, in the same manner and to the same extent as if no such sale had been held.

(c)   Orders for possession of real property sold pursuant to this Article, in favor of the purchaser and against any party or parties in possession at the time of the sale who remain in possession at the time of application therefor, may be issued by the clerk of the superior court of the county in which such property is sold, when:

    (1)   The purchaser is entitled to possession, and

    (2)   The purchase price has been paid, and

    (3)   The sale or resale has been confirmed, and

    (4)   Ten days' notice has been given to the party or parties in possession at the time of the sale or resale who remain in possession at the time application is made, and

    (5)   Application is made to such clerk by the purchaser of the property.

(d)   An order for possession issued pursuant to the preceding subsection shall be directed to the sheriff, shall authorize him to remove the party or parties in possession, and their personal property, from the premises and to put the purchaser in possession, and shall be executed in accordance with the procedure for executing a writ or order for possession in a summary ejectment proceeding under G.S. 42-36.2.

§ 1-339.69. Failure of bidder to comply with bid; resale.

(a)   When the highest bidder at a sale of personal property fails to pay the amount of the bid, the sheriff shall at the same time and place immediately resell the property. In the event no other bid is received, a new sale may be advertised in the regular manner provided by this Article for an original sale.

(b)   When the highest bidder at a sale or resale of real property or any upset bidder fails to comply with the bid within 10 days after the tender to the bidder of a deed for the property or after a bona fide attempt to tender such deed, the clerk of the superior court who issued the execution may order a resale. The procedure for such resale is the same in every respect as is provided by this Article in the case of an original sale of real property.

(c)   A defaulting bidder at any sale or resale or any defaulting upset bidder is liable on the bid, and in case a resale is had because of the default, the defaulting bidder remains liable to the extent that the final sale price is less than the bid plus all costs of the resale or resales. Any deposit or compliance bond made by the defaulting bidder shall secure payment of the amount, if any, for which the defaulting bidder remains liable under this section.

(d)   Nothing in this section deprives any person of any other remedy against the defaulting bidder.

§ 1-339.70. Disposition of proceeds of sale.

(a)   After deducting all sums due him on account of the sale, including the expenses incurred in caring for the property so long as his responsibility for such care continued, the sheriff shall pay the proceeds of the sale to the clerk of the superior court who issued the execution, and the clerk shall furnish the sheriff a receipt therefor.

(b)   The clerk shall apply the proceeds of the sale so received to the payment of the judgment upon which the execution was issued.

(c)   Any surplus shall be paid by the clerk to the person legally entitled thereto if the clerk knows who such person is. If the clerk is in doubt as to who is entitled to the surplus, or if adverse claims are asserted thereto, the clerk shall hold such surplus until rights thereto are established in a special proceeding pursuant to G.S. 1-339.71.

§ 1-339.71. Special proceeding to determine ownership of surplus.

(a)   A special proceeding may be instituted before the clerk of the superior court by any person claiming any money, or part thereof, paid into the clerk's office under G.S. 1-339.70 or G.S. 105-374(q)(6), to determine who is entitled thereto.

(b)   All other persons who have filed with the clerk notice of their claim to the money or any part thereof, or who, as far as the petitioner or petitioners know, assert any claim to the money or any part thereof, shall be made defendants in the proceeding.

(c)   If any answer is filed raising issues of fact as to the ownership of the money, the proceedings shall be transferred to the civil issue docket of the superior court for trial. When a proceeding is so transferred, the clerk may require any party to the proceeding who asserts a claim to the fund by petition or answer to furnish a bond for costs in the amount of $200.00, or otherwise comply with the provisions of G.S. 1-109.

(d)   The court may, in its discretion, allow a reasonable attorney's fee for any attorney appearing in behalf of the party or parties who prevail, to be paid out of the funds in controversy, and shall tax all costs against the losing party or parties who asserted a claim to the fund by petition or answer.

www.ingramcontent.com/pod-product-compliance
Lightning Source LLC
Chambersburg PA
CBHW082112210326
41599CB00033B/6673